May I be filled with loving kindness
May I be well
May I be peaceful and at ease
May I be happy

May the STICK be with you!

JBlack
1/28/10

Published by Five G's Publishing Company
Milledgeville, Georgia

Cover design by Rachel Block
Cover photographs by Kyle Hitchcock

Printed at A&A Printing in Tampa, Florida

First Printing – November 2009

ISBN: 978-0-578-04221-3

Steel Wool on a Stick

my hobby on steroids

Jeff Block

There is a vitality, a life force, a quickening
that is translated through you into action.
Because there is only one of you in all time,
this expression is unique.
If you block it, it will never exist
through any other medium and be lost.
The world will not have it.
It is not your business to determine
how good it is, nor how valuable it is,
nor how it compares with other expressions.
It is your business to keep it yours
clearly and directly, to keep the channel open.
You do not even have to believe in yourself
or your work.
You have to keep yourself open and aware
directly to the urges that motivate you.

Keep the channel open.

~Martha Graham~

Table of Contents

DEDICATION

To my Wife, Deb

*I've lost count of the number of times you
have told me, emailed me and left me notes
saying
"I BELIEVE IN YOU"
Tell me just a few more times
so I might start believing in myself too?*

To my Friend, Jay

*Thanks for 19 years ago showing me how
to twirl a cocktail napkin rose!
Thanks for 19 years of your friendship!*

ACKNOWLEDGEMENTS

*"Putting pen to paper
lights more fire than matches ever will."*
Malcolm Forbes

Bill Quain (www.BillQuain.com) lit *my* fire when I listened to his seminar "The Insider's Secrets for Writing, Publishing and Selling Your Book." Bill is a "blind visionary" who is already encouraging me to write my next book!

Michael Alperstein (www.LuminousLiving.com) did more than just edit my manuscript. He connected deeply with my story and to me personally, providing "spot on" comments, questions, and suggestions. To Michael I say "woo-woo!"

Billy Ashby (www.PrintShopCentral.com) is the reason this book looks so nice. Billy loves book printing!

And a big THANKS to our 30,000+ customers!

I capitalize the words Wife, Husband, Bride, Groom, Mom, Dad, Brother, Sister, Aunt, Uncle, Grandfather, Granddaughters and maybe a few more I've forgotten to list. These are "honorific" titles and all these people deserve to be honored. It's my book and I can capitalize if I want to! My cats* are still cats, not Cats!

*If you find any unusual typos in this book then I must acknowledge our baby cat, Tinkerbell, who just loves to walk across my keyboard while I am typing!

INTRODUCTION

"Do what you love and the money will follow…"
often said by lots of people

"..But NOBODY ever says how far behind
the money follows!"
added by me

YES, we really do sell "steel wool on a stick" for the 11th "steel" Wedding Anniversary! The version on the cover is an old version, but it received great testimonials, lots of "chuckles."   In February 2005, when I created and then sold my very first JustSteelRose, I thought to myself:

"I can't believe I'm selling steel wool on a stick!"

And the title of this book was born.
Ya gotta love niche marketing.

But this book is more than a book about niche marketing.

YES, in 1990 (36 years old) I slept in my car for two days, and no, it wasn't because I enjoy camping out. I was working a commissioned sales job and I was away from my parents' house where I was living. I had $30 to my name and had to choose between gas for my car and food for my belly, or to sleep in a motel. I slept in my car in the motel parking lot and used the shower by the pool to clean up.

Today, *if* I were to sleep in my car, it would be in our 2009 Corvette! You don't believe it? Neither do I! That's why I peek in my garage every night. Yep, there it is!

But this book is more than a book about getting a Corvette.

YES, I have written this book for you. I have read a sizeable bookshelf of self-help books and success stories. I never quite believed them, or at least I closed the back cover saying to myself, "Good story, but 'it' could never happen to me." "It" happened to the author because he/she caught a lucky break, was smart, was handsome or beautiful, met an influential person, had family who encouraged dreams, or had family who financed dreams.

YES, "it" happened to me!

Steel Wool on a Stick is my story. While I would NOT want to travel my path again nor suggest that you take the same road, I will tell you in no uncertain terms that you can go from "where you are" to "where you want to be". I will tell you right here in the introduction that "it" took me 16 years and the end of my story has yet to be written. I started my "journey of 1,000 miles" in 1993 at age 38.

It took me 7 years just to catch up to the starting line!

Now I am living my life based on my own creativity and persistence, living a genuine life, just being me.

YES my business, JustPaperRoses.com, is also just at the starting line as I look forward to doubling or tripling our business in the next few years. But that's not the point. It's my "hobby on steroids". I don't consider what I do to be W-O-R-K. It's just what I do, every day.

There are several things that have happened in my life that I just can't explain. I don't have any religious affiliation, but those of you who do will be comfortable believing that God intervened in my life, more than once. There are mysteries to the way of the Universe that really can't be explained, so I don't search for an explanation. Whatever might be your own belief system I will state with certainty:

YOU ARE MEANT TO BE HAPPY

and if you're not happy, then the path to YOUR own happiness is right before you. Things will happen to YOU too that are beyond explanation!

SO, this book is about YOU, even though the most often used word in this book is "I". What do YOU want? Your dream job? Great marriage? Fast car? World travel?

With passion, persistence and living YOUR genuine life YOU can have it all! I'm writing to you to tell you, if "it" happened to me, then "it" can happen to you.

Envision YOUR life 10 years from now?

Start by reading this book!

Part 1
What I didn't want to be when I grew up

I've always been more than a bit jealous of people who are successful and happy with their careers, who when asked, "When did you know?" answer, "Oh, I've known since I was 10 years old that this is what I wanted to be."

Chapter 1
Little Rhody

*"Son, you get one chance in life to be born wealthy
and you blew it!"*
Dad

We are all framed by our own upbringing whether it is good, bad or ugly. Regardless of one's upbringing there are no guarantees of future success or failure. Some with the roughest of starts rise to great success, and some with the easiest of starts fall way short of their potential.

*"Regardless of your lot in life,
you can build something beautiful on it!"*
Zig Ziglar

Cranston, Rhode Island. Growing up in the smallest State in the Union one develops an "underdog" sense of humor. I knew a few RI facts. RI was smaller than the King Ranch in Texas. Smallest in size yes (1545 sq. miles), but seven States currently have smaller populations. Smallest in size yes, but longest name of any State (Rhode Island and Providence Plantations). In Rhode Island a Sunday afternoon drive could easily become interstate travel! I thought my family owned Block Island, but soon learned we only owned some t-shirts with our namesake.

When I was born in 1954, Providence (next city over) was the costume jewelry manufacturing capital of the world. My Grandfather (maternal) Hy Kleinfeld, owned a jewelry manufacturing business, Star Jewelry Company. My Grandparents and extended family all lived in New York. On November 30, 1947 my Grandfather gained two Son-in-laws at the double wedding of his two Daughters (one was my Mom). Later in this book I'll discuss taking advantage of economies of scale, and I have no doubt that my Grandpa knew he was getting a "deal" by only having to pay for one wedding. Two for the price of one!

By 1952 my Grandfather had brought his "boys", his Son and two Son-in-laws into the business. He shipped my parents off to Rhode Island so my Dad would run the factory while my two Uncles remained in New York to work the showroom, the sales part of the business. My older Brother and Sister were born in New York but I was born in Cranston, yet never had the full Craaaaanston accent because children learn to speak both from their parents and older siblings as well as from their community. Hearing me speak, friends always asked me, "Where are you from?" and were surprised when I answered, "Here."

I don't have any unusual childhood growing up experiences to relate to you and I'll make a point that I'm very much just like the majority of you reading this book. Our family lived in a very middle class family neighborhood of single family homes laid out on rectangular blocks of twelve homes, six side by side in two rows backyard to backyard. I could step out our back door and easily find ten kids ready for play. There was the city municipal field down the street with three baseball/football fields and a public pool. In the winter a second part of the field was flooded and when frozen over it was available for ice skating and hockey. On weekends year round it was not unusual for us kids to be outside from morning through dinnertime on foot, bicycle, or ice skates.

My parents weren't abusive to us or each other. There's only one time I can remember that I was glad I could scramble upstairs to my room faster than my Dad behind me. For the life of me I can't remember my infraction, but I must have deserved at least the threat of a spanking, because my Dad was a gentle and caring Dad. My parents weren't overly doting either. I have no particular stories of inspiration, but there was a constant "do your best" kind of encouragement. My family was just a typical family in the 50s and 60s and my parents kept very busy raising four kids and running a family business.

Okay, come to think of it, here's one inspirational story. July 4th 1961 (I was 6) and we were staying in Plymouth Massachusetts the site of Plymouth Rock, the traditional site of the landing of the Mayflower Pilgrims. The town was having its celebration which included foot races for kids. I was a speedy kid always winning schoolyard races, and my Dad knew this. I was also shy, very shy. The races were on a baseball field and we were standing behind a 4-foot chain-link fence watching when they called my age group. My Dad asked, "Go race?" and I shyly said, "No" (I'd be racing with strangers!). Before I could protest he picked me up and put me over the fence so I had no choice but to line up with all the other little boys. I won! I got a "gold" medal which my Dad had engraved with the date. I lost the medal in one of many moves but the memory of my giddiness in the last 5 yards of the 40-yard race, when I knew I was going to win, is seared in my memory. I guess my Dad was "just do it" long before Nike?

I always knew my parents were doing a little better financially than the neighbors. We had two cars and my Dad traded in and bought a new one every two years. My parents never said "no" when it came to us kids asking to buy something. If there were any money worries at all, my parents kept it private in their bedroom. The only time I ever heard my Dad upset over money was when he was sitting at our dining room table, spread with papers to do his taxes, and a little more than upset as he told my Mom that our dog's vet bills that year totaled more than the doctor bills for his four kids! I think our dog hid for the rest of the weekend.

Now, if your childhood was nowhere as easy as mine, my heart goes out to you. My "walk into the dark forest" started at age 25. I will share more about this, but for now I want to state that YOUR past does not necessarily predict your future. Regardless of your family and childhood circumstances, you can share your gifts with the world, find inner and outer wealth, and create a genuine life for yourself, one that seems effortless. You can begin any time you decide to begin.

> "I felt I was wealthy when I could take my family
> to dinner at our local Chinese restaurant and
> I didn't have to look at the right hand column on the menu"
> Dad

My Dad told me that during the 1950's he and his two Brother-in-laws were each taking $20,000 per year from the business and he added that in those times it was difficult to spend $20,000 per year. He also told me that at its peak Star Jewelry did $2 million in annual sales ($15 million today) and had about 100 employees. The factory started with raw materials coming in the loading dock, and ended with finished packaged jewelry going out the shipping dock to the department stores.

Are business skills genetic? Or learned? Probably both.

At family functions or when my Grandfather or Uncles visited Rhode Island they were always discussing business. I don't recall them ever chatting about sports and they really seemed to enjoy chatting about business in general.

My Grandfather always liked to take a walk around the neighborhood and he usually took me by the hand, telling business stories as we walked, stories that always had a point, a moral to the story. I can remember as early as eight years old wondering, "Why is he telling these stories to an eight year old?" I now recall all of his stories and now understand why he was telling me these stories. The businessmen in my family all instilled in me a respect for a business as an entity of its own to be treated with nurturing care. They all owned businesses.

Family businesses often are "the best of times and the worst of times". In the mid 1960s the costume jewelry industry in Rhode Island was quickly contracting due to importing of jewelry from other countries. My Grandfather retired and his natural Son, my Uncle went off on his own to create a packaging business. My other Uncle was left to get a job in NYC with another jewelry company. My Dad took what was left of the business, consolidated it to a few employees, and he was now selling what other companies manufactured. In 1970 my Dad asked me if I had an interest in the business and I told him "no". My thoughts at the time were to become an Architect or an Engineer and even though I grew up in the family business, I really had no idea what owning and running a business was all about. I didn't know at the time that if I had answered "yes" my Dad would have attempted to hang on to the business even though it wasn't doing so well. He sold out and spent the rest of his career working for other jewelry companies.

My Grandfather did very well. The three "boys" not so well. None of the three were happy with their work after the end of Star Jewelry.

I had good relationships with four men in my family, my Dad, Grandfather, Uncle and Great-Uncle. From my Dad I get my enjoyment of making stuff, manufacturing. From my Grandfather I get my customer service skills. He was a "customer's man" with total focus on gaining a new customer and then creating a satisfied customer. The customer is ALWAYS right! From my Uncle I get my eye towards packaging and presentation. My Great-Uncle told me "be the manufacturer." I now understand his advice. With JustPaperRoses.com we create most of our own products and have no direct competitor, so we're never competing to be "lowest price". Plus we have complete creative control over what we create and sell.

From all four of these men, now deceased, I have a storehouse of wisdom from stories and discussions of business. While I never worked for or with any of them, I consider all four to be my mentors. They would all be proud of what I have created. I too have created a family business, one that hopefully will survive me as I pass it to my Children and Grandchildren. My step-Daughter works for me fulltime, and yes I take walks with my five Granddaughters, and yes I tell them business stories too!

Chapter 2
High School, College & More College

*"Knowledge accumulates in Universities
because freshmen bring a little in
and seniors take none away!"*
Anonymous

No, I didn't go to a school where they teach Origami, but then again I probably folded a thousand paper airplanes while sitting in the back of my classes. I will never disparage my formal education and will always advise and encourage you to attend as many classes and attain as many degrees as possible. But as noted in my comment about one's upbringing, regardless of one's formal education there are no guarantees of future success or failure. No credentials are needed to become a successful entrepreneur.

*"For knowledge add a little every day.
For wisdom subtract a little every day!"*
Lao Tzu

I found my love, career-wise, in 10th grade in front of a drafting board. I was always in the college bound courses, in the top divisions of my grade, but as an elective I thought drafting would be interesting. It was considered a "trade" course so I was in a class with the rougher guys in school. I took to it quickly. This was 1969-1970 before computers, so drafting meant old-school drafting board, t-square, triangles, French curve, pencil and most importantly, eraser. We started at the beginning, learning to draw shapes from different perspectives. We learned the correct way to print letters and numbers. This skill served me well my whole life as my handwriting was so poor I could barely read it, but I learned to print fast, very fast.

One other student and I excelled. It was basically a self-directed curriculum going at our own pace under the guidance of the teacher and the final assignment was "design a house". My progress stalled. It was two weeks before the end of school and I wasn't motivated. The other excellent student spent all his spare time drawing exotic cars and designing other objects. He jumped in and drew his dream house. He became an Architect, someone who can say, "I knew since 10th grade."

I learned that I was great at mimicking and modifying, but not particularly creative when it came to being original. This is more than okay, as you will read that my success with JustPaperRoses.com has been all about mimicking and modifying. There are truly few geniuses in the world with original ideas but many more people who can take those ideas and run with them or morph them, without violating patents, trademarks and copyrights. You do not have to reinvent the wheel in order to be successful. McDonald's did not invent the hamburger, Starbucks did not invent the coffee-house, FedEx did not invent overnight delivery and Netflix did not invent the DVD rental business.

My parents had indulged me with my own drafting table, drafting board and all the tools needed, but they sat idle. 11th Grade came about with a new interest, physics. My teacher was a PhD Mechanical Engineer who had been a college professor and mentioned he was teaching high school to "see what is wrong" with high school physics. I think he really was just between college jobs but it was a great opportunity for us students. His challenge was to "dummy down" teaching physics because his students didn't yet know calculus. For me he did a great job. I loved it. There was one "lesson" I'll never forget. One day in class I was daydreaming (my college major easily could have been "daydreaming in class") and suddenly I heard the teacher shout, "Mr. Block...MOVE!" I snapped out of my dream and looked at him bewildered.

"MOVE!!!" he shouted again and I did a little fidgeting move in my seat. One more time with "MOVE!!!" and I asked him, "Where?" to which he returned to his normal teaching voice saying, "See class, a vector is defined by a force AND a direction." In an informal way he became my mentor. The following year he wrote my recommendations for my college applications for engineering, just like him. I've never forgotten: a vector is a force AND a direction!

14

A few years ago via the internet I found my physics teacher teaching theoretical math at a college and emailed him, retelling the "MOVE" story. I updated him including my schooling of mechanical engineering but not ever becoming a practicing engineer. He responded that he too didn't really like mechanical engineering but found his love with theoretical math. I laughed at the thought of people who might base their career on a mentor only to learn that their mentor wasn't happy with his or her own career!

He also told me that as a teacher he lives for moments like my email to find that his former students are happy doing whatever they are doing, and somehow he was an influence on their lives, even in a small way.

MOVE! In what direction do YOU want to move?

August 1972 and I'm off to Cornell University to study engineering. At this point in my story you might be thinking that I was "advantaged" so therefore of course JustPaperRoses.com would be successful – an Ivy League graduate with all the brains and connections necessary for success, etc. Yes, I had the advantage of a great college education, but as you'll read you'll understand that it didn't work for me. I learned that knowing what you want to be when you grew up is more important than getting good grades. I didn't know what I wanted to be when I grew up. Eventually I started my own business where no college degree was required, not even a Bachelors of Origami!

While I can never be accused of being pragmatic (that's my Wife's job), there were several times in my life where pragmatic solutions turned out to be the best solutions. In my freshman year I took an introductory design course and one of the exercises was to design a tent that weighed no more than 2.5 pounds. The design was simple and once I created the design all I did was take the materials, tent poles and nylon fabric, and just keep reducing the thickness until I got to 2.5 pounds. At this entry level of engineering I could not be sure the tent would even stay up under its own weight, so for a write-up of the exercise I had one paragraph which concluded, "This tent would offer so little protection from the elements that the hiker would be better off sleeping under the stars". I got an A for the assignment.

Also freshman year I had a five minute consideration for walking into the architecture school to inquire about a transfer. I wasn't quite sure I liked engineering, but I knew I liked the idea of becoming an Architect. I put the thought aside when a good friend told me that his brother, who was in the architecture school, was working on his assignments until 2:00 a.m. every morning. Also architecture was a five year curriculum so I viewed a transfer as one that would delay my start of a career. I never made the transfer inquiry. If I had become an Architect I most likely would have been a good journeyman (mimic and modify) but doubt I would have designed award winning structures.

I was what is called an "easy B" student. I didn't have to study much to get a B and would have to study a lot to get an A, so I didn't get a lot of A's. A great opportunity available to some students was the Cornell Engineering work/study program. Participating companies interviewed and offered working internships to students, a chance to make some money, but more importantly a chance to see what engineers really do for a living. I interviewed and got a job offer with Xerox, so in the fall of 1974 I went off to work for four months at their manufacturing facility in Webster, N.Y. Two additional work-blocks were guaranteed for summer of 1975 and summer of 1976.

My internship was as an engineering aide. The first day I walked into a lab where three behemoth Xerox 9200s lived. They were the fastest plain paper copier newly on the market, designed for highest volume runs. This was the first copier to challenge offset printing for black and white high volume print jobs. There were two other full-time engineering aides and I was introduced to them and then told, "This is your machine and there is your tool box".

Machine? Tool box? I was an engineering student. Give me some books with equations to solve, but what's this with a machine and tool box? Are tools in a tool box?

It actually was an interesting job. We were testing various components with different designs and materials. We tested these components in different configurations and temperatures. We would set up for a run, press 999 copies on the control panel and then have about 20 minutes to do

…nothing. One of the aides set up a chess board so we played a lot of chess! After the 20 minutes we would take sample test pages and measure background splatter (clarity and sharpness of the copy) and record several other measurements. Then it was press 999 and play some more chess. At the end of a test run we'd tear down and clean the machine, and set it up for the next test.

One day it was time for me to completely tear down my machine. I had all the parts out, spread on the floor before my machine, when it was quitting time. The next day I put my machine back together, but there were still a few parts on the floor. I was perplexed. Then the other two aides started laughing. Of course they had put some extra parts into my pile! Geek humor at its best?

I had two more internships with Xerox, summer of 1975 and summer of 1976, and enjoyed the money I was making. I had already decided that becoming a practicing career engineer was not for me, not what I wanted to be when I grew up. My boss during the summer of 1975 took a liking to me and advised me to go get my MBA because then at minimum I could come back into engineering but now have the doors opened to management positions. I agreed and also felt relieved because spending two years in an MBA program would give me two more years to figure out what I wanted to be when I grew up.

We were on overtime in the summer of 1976 working 10 hours per day so I got time and a half for 10 additional hours per week. I was newly graduated and newly married, off to MBA school after the summer, so I appreciated the extra money. What didn't make sense was that we didn't have enough to do and the 10 hour days went by real slow. When I asked why we were on overtime the answer was, "Because it's in the budget!" This was my first glimpse of a large company totally wasting money. Another waste was employee theft of small stuff, mostly hand tools. It was almost a company culture to stock one's own home tool box with Xerox tools. The home tool box was probably a Xerox tool box too! A few funny stories circulated. My favorite was of an employee fabricating his own small airplane over many months time using a Xerox machine shop, materials, and his time at work.

Senior year I took four engineering courses to meet the minimum requirements of my degree and I took six courses that would be considered pre-MBA – economics, business and accounting courses.

The University of Chicago MBA program is a home to the efficient market theory and a bastion of free market capitalism. Milton Friedman's "there is no free lunch" originated at U. of Chicago. Our MBA curriculum used the quantitative approach versus the case study approach used by many other MBA programs. Quantitative means highly mathematically and it was a given that those with technical undergrad degrees would fare the best. For me it wasn't a given. Where my engineering math and science left off the MBA program picked up with upper level probability and statistics courses. I got lost in the math.

I did okay, but still didn't know what I wanted to be when I grew up. Courses in production management seemed of interest and I really didn't consider marketing. I ended up with a specialization in finance because I happened to take the course requirements for a specialization in finance.

Similar to my Cornell co-op work/study program I was fortunate at U. of Chicago to get two internships back to back. Internships paid well and were great resume builders. The first internship was working in the computer department at the Inland Steel plant in East Chicago, Indiana for the summer of 1977. It was interesting to learn how steel is actually made (it is f-ing HOT!) but the work was boring and didn't really interest me. We were creating measurement systems and procedures for gathering and analyzing data throughout the steel making process.
It was not what I wanted to be when I grew up.

In order to stay on track for my June 1978 graduation, I took courses in U. of Chicago's night school program while working my two daytime internships. The courses in the night school seemed a little more interesting because the students and some of the professors had day jobs, thus real world experience to bring into classroom discussions. A course was titled "Seminar in Small Business Problems". The professor owned a business that manufactured industrial production counters and timers. He walked in the first night, stood in front of the class chuckling and said, "I just read what they titled my course, 'Seminar in Small Business Problems'. A small business **IS** a problem. Class dismissed!" I enjoyed his class.

He used his own small business for one lesson. Because he was small while his competitors were huge, he could adapt to market changes much quicker than his competitors. His example was the emerging technological for electronic digital counters which made the old mechanical counters obsolete. Another lesson was a "lemons to lemonade" story. Prior to owning his business he had been an executive with a large pots & pans and kitchen utensil manufacturer. He reported to us that some of their new pots and pans had a bottom with an alloy containing a certain metal (I don't remember the particular metal) that was now found to result in pitting from a reaction to salts in food cooked in the pot. He said he was in an airplane sitting next to the marketing VP of the company when it came to him in a flash. He said, "How about if we advertise 'Our pots contain xyz-metal. For proper care, rinse immediately after each use.'" Featuring the metal made it sound more like a benefit, and also increased the perceived value because it sounded exotic and high-end!

Recently in our business we had a terra cotta casting made from our wood "The Kiss" figurine to fill with molten aluminum thus creating an aluminum version of "The Kiss" for the 10th Anniversary. It's a rough terra cotta casting which leaves pits and imperfections. The wording on our site includes "The rough terra cotta casting leaves pits and imperfections but is solid (like your marriage?)."

Thanks Professor!

In the fall of 1977 I started my second internship working at Northwest Industries, Inc., a conglomerate of ten operating subsidiaries with headquarters in the Sears Tower in Chicago, 62nd and 63rd floors. Northwest Industries was the company created in 1968 by Ben Heineman who was President when it was the Chicago & Northwest Railroad company. The railroad was sold and Northwest Industries owned a bunch of industrial companies with approximately $2 billion annual sales. The headquarters was Chicago and the staff in the Sears Tower was about 100 people of which half were MBA's, JD's and other financial specialists. A bunch of smart people, very smart people. In a real sense we were all direct staff to Mr. Heineman, collecting data, analyzing data, and feeding him reports based on our analysis. I was hired as an intern in the Capital Expenditures department where each analyst had an engineering degree and an MBA. Our department was like the "allowance gatekeeper" as projects requiring capital spending over a certain limits had to be approved by headquarters. The fall when I interned was budget season, thus busy season. Our department created a rather detailed Capital Expenditures budget and plan for the next year, on top of our usual workload.

Back at school I had risen to my level of incompetence in an upper level statistics class. The final exam was a take home exam with 24 hours to complete. The data was in three columns – nitrogen content, phosphorous content and burn rate of tobacco leaves. The task was to use regression analysis of the numbers to find the optimum combination of chemicals. This was 1978 and we had shared use of a computer room with now very obsolete computers. I was on the fringe of being clueless and in my first half hour couldn't seem to get anything but an answer of 1-part to 1-part derived from a very simple regression. I looked around the computer room to my classmates to see all of them working feverishly. These were computer-tape fed computers which have a teletype sound to them, so the room was literally buzzing with activity. I gave up after six hours figuring I might actually get an F on this one. I was the first of my classmates to leave the computer room. Pragmatism struck once again. I wrote a paragraph answer that the results were optimal at a simple ratio of 1 to 1, and concluded that "sometimes the simplest is the best".

I got an A and was the only one with the correct answer!

In a marketing class where an assignment was to be completed with a partner I met a student who was, for his own interest, using the school's computers to model the daily market prices of the silver market. I was curious and interested so he and I teamed up to expand the computer model. The U. of Chicago had a DEC-20 which at the time was the biggest and baddest computer in town. We were allocated "funny money" time on the computer and our simulation burned it at a fast rate. We started asking for and getting computer "funny money" from other students who had no use for the computer that quarter.

We were introduced by a professor to a young and successful commodity trader in town, Tom Dittmer. In 1978 Tom was in a small office with maybe 30 employees.

His company was REFCO started by his step-Dad. My student friend and I walked into his office and Tom started with "OK, what do you guys want?" to which my partner started pulling out computer sheets and started talking about our simulation of the silver market. Tom stopped him quickly saying, "I know what you're going to show me looks great, so I don't need to see your computer sheets. What do you need to test it?" I said, "$10,000" and he raised his voice and said, "Gail, come in here with an account form". Then Tom asked, "OK, what's the split?" and I responded, "We thought it would be 20% for us, 10% each, and 80% for you since it's your money." Tom said, "Nah, that's too complicated. Let's make it 1/3, 1/3, 1/3." Just before we left his office he reached under his desk and came out with two copies of a book that was printed on yellowed paper, like an old Bible. The book was "Reminiscences of a Stock Operator" by Edwin Lefèvre. Tom had a case of them under his desk and handed one to everyone he met, or maybe just to naïve students!

I hope you keep a case of this book under your desk too!

Things ended rather strangely when I got called into his office and he told me he wanted to end our relationship. I think my partner had said something to him but I'll never know what happened. The trading program had made money but was very erratic. At the moment we were ahead $2400 and Tom cut checks for $1200 for me and $1200 for my partner (none for himself) and we were done.

But it was time for graduation and entrance into the real world. I had been offered and accepted a full-time job at Northwest Industries, my same job as an intern but now as an analyst in the Capital Expenditures department.

My Grandfather asked me, "What is happening to all the entrepreneurs today?" and I responded "Grandpa, they've offered me $19,500 (1978 dollars) guaranteed! Why should I risk my money?" It seems that 31 years later, now *everybody* wants to be an entrepreneur and the days of an almost guaranteed career in the corporate world are over.

June 1978 brings graduation at University of Chicago Graduate School of Business and at commencement there was a typical "there is no free lunch" speech by the Dean. I had borrowed $14,000 to learn "there is no free lunch"?

Yes, in the real world there is no free lunch. Everything that comes our way has a cost, paid for with time, energy, and/or money.

My "formal" education ended.

I still didn't know what I wanted to be when I grew up.

Chapter 3
Oh No! Not the Real World!

"If you don't know who you are,
the markets are an expensive place to find out!"
anonymous

So, is figuring out what we want to be when we grow up really a process of eliminating what we don't want to be? What happens if we keep eliminating and never find what we want to be? I KNOW I am not the only person who is a late bloomer. I'm just real happy I finally bloomed!

"The five happiest people I have ever met
all had this strange little quirk
of referring to their jobs as a 'calling'."
Eric Sevareid

My career at Northwest Industries started off good. Everything was new, I was making money, and there was to be a small amount of business travel too. My peers from school who hired into consulting firms were traveling all around the world to exotic locations. My first business trip was to Los Angeles and I had images in my head of Disneyland and Hollywood. "Los Angeles" turned out to be an industrial city called Fullerton, and we spent a week of 10 hour days in a conference room without windows. But the work was interesting. By the time a capital request got to us at headquarters it had already been worked up by the operating company and approved by signature of the President of the operating company. Our direct contact with an operating company was always with the President and/or top department heads. Generally an operating company overstated the cost savings from a new piece of equipment or new process, so we reanalyzed everything with a little different set of parameters, but rarely denied a request for expenditure.

The pyramid at Northwest Industries was very flat. I reported to my boss, who reported to the VP of Finance, who reported to Mr. Heineman. There was no clear path to promotions although the man who used to be in my boss's position was now the President of an operating company. Also the man who used to be the special assistant to Mr. Heineman was now a President of an operating company. I got promoted "quickest ever" in six months to Senior Analyst and when I asked about my pay raise was told that would come at my annual review. I'm not sure why I got promoted because my responsibilities were the same and my pay was the same. A few months later, after Mr. Heineman had selected a new special assistant, I was told I had been on his "short list" of candidates!

We were in the 3-piece suit era and I was working in a beautifully furnished office. My cubicle was three sided and open to a traffic isle with a view of grey filing cabinets. I'm not sure who I was dressing up for. After working one year it was again time to start creating the new budget, my third budget season. It was getting boring and repetitious.

In a passing conversation another employee told me he was trading silver futures on a small exchange called the MidAmerica Commodity Exchange. He would go on the trading floor during lunchtime, trade for an hour, and then come back to work. I checked it out. The MidAmerica was a secondary market to the Chicago Board of Trade and the Chicago Mercantile Exchange, and traded what was called mini-contracts. For example the BOT had a 5000 bushel corn contract and the MidAmerica had a 1000 bushel corn contract. Similarly with silver, where BOT and the COMEX in NYC had 5000 ounce contracts and the MidAm had a 1000 ounce contract. I went on the floor as a visitor a few times. I was hooked.

I borrowed money from my Grandfather to purchase a membership but for trading money I was on my own. The membership cost about $12,000 and I had about $3,000 for a trading account. Yep, I was one of those guys you see in the trading pits, screaming and waving their arms.

The function of a floor trader who is trading with his/her own money is to provide liquidity to a market, always willing to buy or sell for a price. When a trader buys on his bid and sells on his offer it's called "getting the edge". When you buy and sell all day long, hopefully getting the edge on most trades, you end up grinding out a profit sometimes called "scalping the market". A pure and very simplified example is say the last posted price for Gold is $900 per ounce. A floor broker handling customer orders gets an order to buy a contract of Gold "at the market". He's in the trading pit and shouts out, "900 for Gold" and a market maker responds back "at 901". The broker shouts back, "SOLD" and the transaction takes place at 901. The price ticker to the world now says 901. Next a broker gets an order to sell a contract of Gold "at the market" so he shouts out, "Sell Gold at 901" to which the market maker responds, "900 for Gold" and the broker shouts "SOLD". The price ticker to the world now shows 900 as the last price traded. The market maker just sold a contract at 901, then bought a contract at 900 creating a $1 per ounce profit (each futures contract is 100 ounces), almost risk free.

I started trading during my lunch hour, and most days my hour became an hour and a half, then two, sometimes two and a half. When I got back to my desk at Northwest Industries my afternoons were **always** bad. If I had made $300 during lunch, I was excited and de-motivated to work. If I lost $300 during lunch, I was down and de-motivated to work. I now had one foot in the door, and one foot out the door of Northwest Industries.

After a few short months I was about even from my lunchtime trading but the handwriting was on the wall – it was time for me to be a full time trader. I strongly believed that a floor trader was what I wanted to be when I grew up!

At the one year mark of being in the real world my Wife graduated law school and started her career. Six months later it appeared her income could handle our bills, so I quit Northwest Industries and began trading full time in January of 1980. After three months I was dead even and frustrated. I understood in theory how to "scalp" a market. I observed a few of the better traders on the floor and knew they weren't doing anything I couldn't do. A friend who was an established floor trader at the Chicago Mercantile Exchange told me to start trading the back month spreads. Futures traders buy and sell contracts that are specified by future delivery months. The further out months are called back months and the liquidity gets worse the further out you go, so therefore the bid/ask spread gets wider and more profitable. When I bought or sold a back month it was important to quickly offset the trade by an opposite trade of a front month to try to lock in a profit.   If I were sharp and quick, knowing the current spread price between trading months, I could make a nice profit trading the back month spreads. I was sharp and quick with math.

The next three months I made money almost every day. In my best month I made money 18 of 21 trading days. I started trading more contracts at a time and started getting a little respect in the pit. But I was also getting too big for my britches. I was up about $8,000 in those three months, so an annualized $32,000 compared to my $20,000 salary at Northwest Industries! I was a small (but growing) fish in a small pond, but next door was the Chicago Board of Trade and down the street was the Chicago Mercantile Exchange where it was not unusual for floor traders to make several hundred thousand dollars per year, or even a million or two. The parking garages around the main two exchanges were like exotic or luxury car showrooms.

I didn't notice that it was a bad thing that I was smoking a joint on the way to work each day. In fact I thought it was a good thing. My math skills didn't seem impaired, so I smoked on the way to work and during work too. Traders and exchange employees were active marijuana and cocaine users and abusers, with the wealthier ones being more into cocaine. I liked my reefer. If I didn't have any of my own all I had to do was step into a back fire escape stairwell at the exchange and share with someone smoking there, or pick up a roach or two left behind on the floor. There were many days when I thought the smoke in the fire escape stairwell would set off a fire alarm!

Another symptom I didn't notice, or did notice but justified, was that I was carrying market positions overnight. The least risky strategy would be to close out or spread off positions at the end of the day to go home relatively neutral. But I started speculating. If I was right and the next morning the market opened in my direction then it was a quick start to a good day. If I was wrong and the next morning the market opened in the wrong direction then it was a quick start to a bad day.

I had played a fair amount of friendly poker in college and I know that I was a net loser. I liked to watch my hands develop and stayed in too many hands hoping to be dealt a long shot winning hand. In poker "ya gotta know when to fold em". The same goes for trading. A trader has to pick his spots and if he's wrong quickly get out and take a small loss before it becomes a big loss. I wasn't very good at "fold em." I was treating my floor trading like gambling.

Then one day "it" happened – no, not a good "it" at all. I lost about $3,000 in one day and was overtrading my means. The next day and the next I came back with a vengeance to regain my losses and just added more losses. My Mercantile Exchange trader friend voiced his concern as he advised me to "just trade onesies". I agreed.

The next morning I entered the trading floor determined to limit my trading to onesies or twosies. The opening bell sounded and a broker shouted out a trade, I said, "SOLD" and he turned to me and asked, "25?" meaning would I take 25 contracts? I said, "No, 10" and it was the beginning of the end. By the end of the day I had lost $3,000 more than existed in my trading account. It's difficult to express that at that moment I had begun my walk into the dark forest. My mind was short-circuiting, and it was very painful.

I knew I couldn't simply borrow money and go back to conservative trading. I had failed. The only solution would be to sell my membership to pay off what I owed on the trading account. I "busted out", something that happened to other floor traders too, somewhat too often.

I left the exchange in a fog and when I turned a corner around a building a homeless man asked me for a dollar. I almost belted him. I just lost more money than I had, plus I lost my livelihood a mere half-hour before. I went to my Wife's office and broke down crying. My Wife had known I was having some bad days, but this was a huge shock to her, and to our marriage.

The next few months were agonizingly, horribly painful. I contemplated suicide for the first time. "Contemplated" is a step below "planning" which is a step below "doing". We lived on the 12th floor of a condo building and more than once I eyed the small window as my means of escape. Contemplated includes all the mental anguish of someone who is suicidal. Contemplated means envisioning suicide.

I didn't know what to do. I thought I knew what I wanted to be when I grew up (a floor trader), but I had crashed and burned just heading into the very first turn. I became fixated on "getting back to the MidAm". I started looking in help wanted ads. I probably sent my resume to companies who hire U. of Chicago MBAs, but I had really fallen off the MBA "fast track". I felt unsuitable to dress up in a suit again. I saw an ad for hiring of commodity futures account executives, hired on, and found myself in a "smile and dial" telephone sales job. I hated it. The company was always in trouble with customers. I created a few of my own issues with customers too.

Nobody is happy when they lose money in the markets.

I called on someone I knew from the MidAm trading floor who I had heard was now off the floor and had established a small brokerage business. His office was under the umbrella of a well established but also small clearing company which was a member of all the exchanges. I started working there in January 1982.

I got fortunate in a few ways but one was in finding a partner. Partnerships work out best when the division of the tasks is clear. In our case it was easy. I brought in the business and my partner handled it once it was in. So we shook hands on a 50/50 deal and got to work. I also got fortunate in that we were in the right time and right place for the discounting of commissions.

I realize only now as I write this 26 years later, that being able to discount was an "inch of daylight" and a breath of fresh air for me. Our customers were people, mostly men, who were trading in the market calling their own shots. In 1983 we would offer them $35 per trade and for many it was a no-brainer since they might be paying as much as $100 per trade elsewhere. Our clearing firm would split 50/50 with us on the $35 so we'd get $17.50 per trade and my partner and I would split again, so we'd each get $8.75 per trade. Customers who trade with discount commissions generally were more active (and more active than they should have been) so it was not difficult to build our income with just 15 to 20 active customers.

A good partnership also becomes more than just the sum of its parts. In our case it freed me up to just sell, sell, sell.

A single person account executive hits a glass ceiling too soon. You start with no customers so all you have to do is sell. But when you start getting customers, handling their accounts starts eating into your selling time. 1983 through 1986 were good years. My partner and I began making about $2,500 per month and it was consistent. I had brought in a small army of customers who did their own trading and my partner's phone was always ringing.

In the introduction of this book I mentioned "things I just can't explain". Well here's one of them:

My Wife and I planned to have a baby. We found out she was pregnant in September 1983. Up until then my partner and I had each been making about $2,500 per month.

***In September 1983 my monthly income doubled,
to $5,000 like a switch had been turned on!***

Now I know the increase was based on the work I had done over the previous several months, but suddenly, just as I learn I'm going to be a Daddy, more accounts were coming in. A few of our active customers became more active too.

In the winter of 83/84 there was a day in Chicago when it was -28° with a -80° wind chill factor. I actually walked from my building to a friend's building a few blocks away for a poker game and almost froze on the way and way back. My Wife and I had already discussed moving to Florida and -28° made the decision an easy one!

We decided to stay in Chicago through the coming spring, summer and fall and move just before Thanksgiving 1984.

For our New Year's 1984 "resolution" my partner and I agreed that we'd like to see one month in 1984 where we each made $10,000. It turned out that we had several months where we made at least $10,000! This was a very good thing for an expectant Dad! When the due date in May of 1984 approached I found myself with some cash in my pocket after too long of a dry spell. We bought all the baby stuff and didn't have to scrimp.

Our Daughter was born in May of 1984. I printed her birth announcement on a Macintosh computer I had bought a few months after they were introduced by Apple. It was an amazing machine and leap of technology for its time. It had a mouse! I used it as a word processor to print marketing letters for work. I also had fun playing with the graphics which were then printed on a dot matrix printer.

In June of 1984 there was a change of ownership of the clearing firm and my partner and I decided to not stay on with the new owners. At this time we had a very nice book of business to take with us, so we found another clearing firm and brought most of our customers with us. I worked there until November when we moved to sunny Florida.

I still didn't know what I wanted to be when I grew up.

At about the same time many companies were competing with discounted commissions below our $35 per trade. If I wasn't quoting lower prices, the conversation with a prospective customer ended quickly. Also at $35 per trade we were at the lower limit of where the clearing firm would be okay with a 50/50 split. We could quote lower prices, but we'd make less too. I learned that if price is your only feature it becomes a very tough sale, of course unless you are the lowest price. We weren't the lowest price.

I became cynical about the entire industry of "the markets". To the individual customer it really is white collar gambling. The University of Chicago MBA teaches the efficient market theory which basically says that today's price reflects all that is known today. The market moves based on changing information and/or changing opinions but these changes are not predictable. But there's a whole financial industry that in some way or another is in the game of "beat the market". Advertisements for brokerage houses all imply quite clearly that your money can do better when it's with them. And the media feeds into it. Daily, if not hourly, financial news reports pin a "reason" on to every fluctuation of a market no matter how small.

"On Wall Street today, news of lower interest rates sent the stock market up, but then the expectation that these rates would be inflationary sent the market down, until the realization that lower rates might stimulate the sluggish economy pushed the market up, before it ultimately went down on fears that an overheated economy would lead to a reimposition of higher interest rates."

Mankoff (cartoon) The New Yorker Magazine 1981

Ask yourself this two part question:
a) If somebody really could beat the market, wouldn't
ALL investors put their money with him or her?
b) If somebody really could beat the market, why would
they tell YOU?

Our customers ran the gamut from seat of the pants
decision makers to those with all sorts of systems. It's so
tempting. A glance of almost any chart of price movement
has even me seeing patterns. But almost all individual
traders lose money. The institutional traders who do make
money do so because they take positions as market makers
and/or they're brokering deals on a fee or commission
basis. If it really is just a big casino, then the "house" take
is all the commissions and fees. It's a huge number. Huge!
Las Vegas was not built with the winners' money. Same
goes for "the markets". The industry has thousands of
ways for you to "invest" and every time there is a charge.
It's basically a zero sum game with the house taking money
off the table with each and every hand.

In November of 1984 we moved to Florida and I became
an early pioneer of working from home – the home office.
The internet hadn't yet been invented but my business was
all on the telephone and my customers really didn't care
where I was. My partner was in Chicago handling their
accounts so nothing changed there. For a few months
I made telephone calls like I did in Chicago, but I was
producing no results and my attitude was bad and getting
worse. I knew that business already in house wouldn't last

forever and I wasn't finding new customers to replace those who lost their money and closed their accounts.

I had a severe case of "I can't" for doing something different. Everything suggested by family or friends was not what I wanted to be when I grew up. Also the income would be starting-at-the-bottom income. I had just recently had a year where I made over $80,000 (1984) so how could I start at the bottom? In hindsight I should have started a pool cleaning company. Florida was adding houses and pools every day. I'd be the first employee cleaning the first pools. But my "I can't do that" had me stuck protesting, "I can't clean people's pools for a living." If my thinking wasn't so stinking, this book would probably be titled:

Jump In, The Water Is Fine!
How I cleaned up by cleaning 100,000 pools!

My marriage was stressed and not doing well. My Wife was (and still is) an attorney and the rent was paid and food was on our table. I enjoyed much of 1984 through 1988 as a "Mr. Mom" caring for our baby Daughter while also trying to figure out what I wanted to be when I grew up. My depression was constant and getting worse. I continued smoking a lot of marijuana. I really needed no help to beat myself up, feeling so guilty for being over 30 without a career. My family and few friends were as supportive as could be, but nobody else could provide a "cure". It's not easy to be married to someone like me or someone who was going through what I was going through. I would not want to be married to myself either. I was a walking mess.

My Wife and I separated in August of 1988 and divorce followed a few months later. From 1988 through 1991 I would stumble from job to job, grasping at anything that looked like it could produce a paycheck. My jobs included commissioned sales jobs selling for a health club, dating service, arcade games vendor, executive recruiter, infomercial promoter, two adjustable bed companies, and a few I've probably forgotten. All of the sales jobs required memorizing a script and following a prescribed procedure. The goal was to separate a customer from their money. All were "selling the sizzle, not the steak".

These businesses didn't even have a steak. I fizzled.

My non-sales jobs were driving for a limo company for one winter season and working as a crew member for a carpet cleaning company.

I certainly didn't know what I wanted to be when I grew up and none of these jobs during this time period even qualified me to say I was "searching".

I wasn't searching.

I should have invented GPS because, I was lost!

Chapter 4
Jeff's Angels

"All God's angels come to us disguised."
James Russell Lowell

We usually do not know when an Angel has just walked into our lives. It's only with hindsight can we see how certain people impacted our lives and understand the gifts they brought to us. But Angels do arrive. I've met three.

"You'll meet more angels on a winding path
than on a straight one."
Daisey Verlaef

March of 1990 and I had just quit driving for a limo company as the Florida winter season slowed down and my depression was in high gear. I was done, cooked, looking for a way out of my misery. My "out" as a child was a fantasy of running away to Australia. Of course as a child I never even ran away across the street. So now I booked a ticket to Australia. I was living on my credit cards, approaching my limits totaling about $35K, and I cash-advanced the last $6K to see me to Australia. What I was going to do there I had no idea, but I had no plans to come back. My ticket was for June.

I was living in a rented a room in a private house in Boca Raton, a nice set up with a private entrance to my room and bathroom. Boca Raton is home to many wealthy people, but like most wealthy communities there's also a large population of "mere" working people, with houses and apartments for their budgets too.

In April I was at my somewhat regular bar & grill, standing at the bar when a couple squeezed in next to me, her next to me and her guy on the other side. The two of them started exchanging dirty jokes and I jumped in with a few of my own. Jay introduced himself and his friend, and over the course of the night Jay and I compared notes and found we were both divorced and my almost 6 year old Daughter was age-wise right between his two Daughters of 4 and 7. Since we were both seeing our Daughters every other weekend we synchronized weekends and over the next few months we enjoyed each other's company with our girls.

On weekends when Jay and I didn't have our girls, or on weeknights, he and I would go out as two "wild and crazy" single guys. Unfortunately, we weren't particularly good at being either wild or crazy! Or maybe fortunately?

At another bar I watched as Jay grabbed a cocktail napkin and started doing something with it around his fingers. When he finished, there it was! A cocktail napkin rose! No I didn't hear Angels (or Jay) sing, or even a trumpeting fanfare, but I loved what I saw. I fumbled around under Jay's instruction and started making good ones after the fourth or fifth attempt. Hmmm, single, broke, and now I had a FREE flower to make for the ladies!

Jay was an Angel walking in to my life, delivering a cocktail napkin rose. In hindsight when he first handed me a cocktail napkin rose it was like the passing of a torch, but I never would have guessed it would be the seed of a future business! Some seeds take many years to germinate!

So, who says you can't meet nice people in a bar?

During my years as a single guy I twirled hundreds of cocktail napkin roses (see photo on the back cover). On our website we created a 16 page PDF with photos, titled "Paper Flowers, Sex and the Single Guy". It has instructions for twirling a cocktail napkin rose and also for folding an Origami flower, plus a guide to flirting with a cocktail napkin rose. Guys, this works! And no, I will not provide details upon request!

But my favorite story of a cocktail napkin rose fast forwards us to 2006 when my second (and last!) Wife and I went to dinner at a restaurant in Ft. Lauderdale. While waiting for a table we sat at the bar. There were two women seated next to my Wife and closest one announced to the bartender that she was celebrating her 62nd birthday. Hearing this I took a cocktail napkin and twirled a rose. I reached across in front of my Wife, tapped the birthday girl on her shoulder and when she looked I presented her with the cocktail napkin rose and said, "Happy Birthday!" She looked, took the rose and asked, "Did you just make this?" I made another rose while she watched and I also narrated with the shortened version of this book, my story of making paper roses for a living. I gave her my business card too, which has a photograph of JustPaperRoses®. She was in awe, captivated watching my fingers at work and listening to my story. When I was done I reached out and again handed her this second cocktail napkin rose. She took it in her hand, paused, then looked my Wife directly in her eyes and asked, "Do *you* do anything?…besides him?"

I couldn't and still can't stop laughing!

Back to May, 1990. And then there was Sally. The next month after meeting Jay, same bar a little less crowded. I had finished my dinner at the bar and turned around to face the crowd. Almost like the "Moses effect", for a moment the people parted and I see a pretty blonde walking right up to me. I thought she was going to lean in next to me to order something from the bartender, so I was taken off guard when she came up to me face to face, introduced herself and asked me to join her and her two girlfriends at a table on the other side of the restaurant. I did. When I sat down the introductions included that Sally was a pharmaceutical rep and both her friends were in medical related fields. I joked, "I'm not a doctor but I've been mistaken 7 or 8 times around Boca for a Dr. L*" Sally asked, "Girls, does he look like Dr. L?" and Sally added, "do this" motioning a hand across the mouth the way a doctor would look wearing a surgical mask. I put my hand across my mouth and they all said "nah" and giggled.

*Name changed. For the past several months 7 or 8 different people had mistaken me for Dr. L, saying "Hi L" or "Hi Dr. L" to me. One couple even got a few sentences into a conversation before I said, "You must be mistaking me for Dr. L"!

That night we all went to a movie and then I went home with Sally. The next day we were in her apartment swimming pool, standing with our arms around each other, talking, and she said, "You're not all here." I asked, "What do you mean?" She went on, "Your mind isn't all here. You're somewhere else." My floodgates burst. We spent the next three hours holding each other and she wouldn't let me go. We both got badly sunburned.

I told Sally of my plans for Australia, my lack of a job or career, my financial indebtedness and all my woes. She assured me in no uncertain terms that everything would be okay, *like she knew it for a fact!* When we went back upstairs to her apartment she went into her kitchen and came back out approaching me with a pill in one hand and a glass of water in her other hand and said, "take this"

as she literally put the pill in my mouth. It was Prozac.
I really didn't know what Prozac was, but I swallowed it.
I trusted Sally. YES, Sally should NOT have given me
prescription medicine. It is not the right thing to do unless
one is a doctor who is prescribing for his/her patients.

BUT, sometimes Angels have to use unorthodox methods.

Sally saved my life.

The next day Sally drove me to the airport and gave me no
option but to cash in my ticket to Australia. The next few
weeks I stayed with Sally and continued daily on Prozac.
She stayed very close by as my body adapted to the
medication, which included a few days of the "shakes".

And then? Then the clouds started to clear.

There's a fair amount of opinion that anti-depressants can
cause suicide. I can only report of my own personal
experience. During the first few weeks being on Prozac
my thoughts, now starting to clear, focused on, "oh shit,
my life REALLY IS as bad as I thought it was, and maybe
even worse!" I think the expression "reality sucks" was
coined by someone in the early stages of antidepressant
medication. In my opinion and personal experience
suicidal thoughts are there before antidepressants, and the
same suicidal thoughts are there after antidepressants.

So, I don't blame the antidepressants.

My relationship with Sally ended, but not before she told me that the REASON she approached me in the bar that night was BECAUSE I looked like Dr. L, a man whom she had dated and for whom she still had feelings! She also told me she almost passed out that first night in the bar when it was <u>I</u> who brought up his name!!!

I can't explain it:

Sally walks up to me because I look like someone else and ends up being one of my Angels?

Was Jay sent to me?
Was Sally sent to me?

Chapter 5
Westward Ho!

"Sometimes what a man escapes to
is worse than what he escapes from."
Stan Lynde

A geographic fix probably would have worked for me if only I didn't have to tell myself where I was going!

"Travel makes a wise man better
but a fool worse!"
Thomas Fuller

I found a doctor who prescribed Prozac for me. I had no job, little money, no place to live and now I was not running away to Australia. My new friend Jay was part-owner of a chain of video stores and I turned to him to ask for a job. He said, "I have to tell you two things. First, I have partners so I can only pay you what we pay everyone else." I responded, "That's fine I just need something, anything to do." Jay continued, "Second, I'm different at work than I am socially." I responded, "I sure hope so!"

I started working for Jay and fortunately my parents were up north for the summer and fall, so I could live in their house rent free and by myself. Jay's stores were just starting with computerizing the inventory of video tapes (this was pre-barcode era) and my job was to spend a few days in each store assigning each tape a numerical code and entering it into the store's computer. This job ended when Jay and his partners sold out to Blockbuster Video in August 1990. I guess I could have stayed on with a store clerk job but decided to look for something else, hopefully where I could make more money. Unemployed again!

I saw an ad in the newspaper for commissioned sales, called the phone number and went to a hotel for a mass hiring and training of salespeople for Niagara Adjustable Beds. It turns out that Niagara, headquartered in Escondido California, was owned by a "defector" from Craftmatic Adjustable Beds (Florida) who, along with other past Craftmatic salesmen, was aggressively targeting the same markets. The training was very high energy.

Hundreds responded, probably about 50 showed up for training and maybe 25 survived the training. The sales trainers were so good that if I had the money, I would have bought a bed from them myself!

The sale is an in-home sale and I was not very good at it. Niagara would send me on 1 to 3 appointments per day and they each could be 60 miles apart. We were trained for a three hour presentation. The expectation of the company was every appointment would be a sale, no excuses.

Even today I have a mixed opinion on the business. Yes, it's a "high pressure" in-home sale, but I'm not even sure what "high pressure" is, and I was there, myself. Many of the customers were eager to buy the bed and had wanted one for many years. More than a few customers with various ailments or bad backs were sleeping every night in their recliner chairs because that was their only comfortable position. An adjustable bed duplicated the recliner chair position. If my Dad were sleeping in a recliner would I "high pressure" him to buy an adjustable bed? You bet I would. Affordability and price are different issues. Were the customers buying an overpriced bed? Yes. Would they go out on their own to price shop and then buy a less expensive brand? Most likely not.

The appointment setters promised a free gift for just sitting through the presentation and that was why many said "yes" to the appointment. Others were just lonely senior citizens who enjoyed having any company at all in their home.

I was in homes where cash or credit was just not possible and in such bad shape (home and occupant both) that I would have bought them a bed myself, if I could.

So I survived, including sleeping in my car two nights when Niagara had me on the west coast of Florida for appointments. I had $30 to my name and had to choose between gas for my car and food for my belly, or to sleep in a motel. I slept in my car in the motel parking lot and used the shower by the pool to clean up each morning.

Almost all businesses that use outside commissioned salespeople have inside sales managers. I learned that if a salesperson survived a few months there would be almost nobody left from their training class, and thus you can be a candidate to move inside to be an inside sales manager. The inside sales manager is the umbilical cord for the outside salesperson doing the in-home sale. The procedure of selling includes a call in to the office and as a last resort, if necessary, putting the customer on the phone with an inside sales manager who tries to close the deal. I spoke with the manager in Escondido and asked if I came out there, would there be a position for me as an inside sales manager, and he said "yes".

During the entire time period of 1988 through 1991 I was scraping bottom and never getting off the bottom. I had only the cash in my pocket, a car payment, mounting credit card debt, child support that I couldn't pay, and depression that never let up for an instant. A real mess. Not the kind of man you want **your** Daughter to bring home!

My move to Escondido was another "escape". I packed *everything* I owned into my Plymouth Laser (Mitsubishi Eclipse) and put my bicycle on a bike rack too. I had a teary goodbye with my 6 year old Daughter telling her I wasn't sure if I'd ever be back. My mentality always had the back door option of "if this next job doesn't work out I'll just commit suicide". The job in Escondido would pay $500 per week and I could split rent of a two bedroom apartment with another of the inside managers (there were about ten of us) whose roommate had just moved out. I drove cross country in January 1991 in two days of almost non-stop driving. We live in a beautiful country.

Escondido is about 40 miles north of San Diego and in Spanish means "hidden". A great place for me to hide? It's a small city of about 100,000 people set in a valley surrounded by what they call hills, but to this Floridian used to flat terrain they were mountains. We worked six day weeks and on my seventh day I was always on my bicycle. The five main roads out of Escondido were all, of course, uphill climbs. The downhill rides after the crest were exhilarating and dangerously fast. I wore out a set of brakes every two months. I also learned to use all ten speeds whereas in Florida I only needed two. After a month I decided to see if I could bicycle to Solana Beach on the Pacific Ocean which is 17 miles from Escondido. Of course if I bicycled there I'd have to do the return trip too, so it was a 34 mile ride. It was a great all day ride which I repeated several more times after the first time.

While my fitness between my ears was the worst, my physical fitness was the best. Fortunately I'm the type of person who exercises in reaction to stress, anxiety and depression. I noticed I was getting great bicyclist thighs from my workouts, plus the scenery was magnificent.

The fitness between my ears got worse and worse. I was taking Prozac which I'm sure was helping, but I sought no counseling and I was isolated from any contact with friends or family. The only socializing I did was Friday or Saturday nights at the Belly Up Tavern in Solana Beach (discovered on my first bicycle trip to the beach) where they had live music and two pool tables. We had a pool table in our basement when I was a kid, and I was now a fairly good shot. I found shooting pool to be about the only activity where my brain could focus on something other than my misery, and my game sharpened. One night at the Belly Up, I defeated about 25 challengers staying on the table all night long for the cost of my original 50 cents!

I survived for seven months at Niagara but was on the "outs" with the owner, where all the other inside managers were on the "in". I seem to have a way of not buying into the bullshit of others and I guess (no, I know) I don't hide it well. He fired me. About the same time I got a phone call from someone about my lack of my past eight months of car payments, and he said he was just looking for an "updated billing address". I got stupid and gave him my new address. The next morning my car was gone from the apartment parking lot.

Unemployed, no money, no car and rent due in two weeks. I still had my bicycle. My thoughts were to take one last bicycle ride to the beach and when I got to the ocean I'd just keep going. This was now the second time in my life where I was deep into contemplation of suicide and the emotional pain was intense. Very intense. Very painful.

Then something happened which I just cannot explain.

I decided I had to get back to Florida. It was not an option to ask my parents for money to get back east. They had already helped me as much as they could and at this moment in their lives they were going through some financial drains from other family issues. I knew there were companies that needed drivers to drive cars to various destinations so I opened up the Yellow Pages and called one of them. My thought was just to get anywhere on the east coast as close to Florida as possible. A woman answered and after a three minute chat she felt I was responsible enough. I had told her I was looking to get to Florida. She asked, "Do you know where Boca Raton is?" and my heart skipped a beat, maybe more than one beat. I told her, "Sure do!" A woman needed her car driven from San Diego to Boca Raton and she'd only have a few of her things in the back seat, so I could use the trunk and the rest of the car for my stuff! Then I got the destination address. A journey of **2,635 miles** and with **one phone call** I would land **within 1 mile** of a friend who could give me a ride back to my parents' house! "Ask and thou shall receive?" Another Angel? An Angel I never met, loaned me her car!

Three days later I was back in Florida!

I had no choice but to file for bankruptcy. My own debts were about $40K and I had no light at the end of the tunnel for paying it off. My ex-Wife had filed for bankruptcy the year before and now our jointly owned townhouse, where she no longer lived, became my obligation too.

September 1991, bankrupt, no job, and living with my parents again. I called up a man who had trained me with Niagara who I knew was now working back at Craftmatic as a manager of the inside managers. I was desperate for any income, so I interviewed and got hired doing the same thing I did at Niagara, and I hated it just as much.

In October I saw an ad in the newspaper for a sales and marketing manager for a "South Florida subsidiary of a Fortune 500 company" and one of the requirements was an MBA. I typed up my resume and included a cover letter with a 2" x 3" photograph. The year before my Mom had scheduled and paid for a professional photo shoot, insisting that I get dressed in a suit and tie and my then 6 year old Daughter get dressed in a pretty flowery dress. I obliged reluctantly (I'm not a suit and tie kind of guy) with an "oh Mom" type of attitude.

To my resume and cover letter I attached an outdoor shot of my Daughter posed standing in front of me. My cover letter started with, "Attached is my resume and photograph (I'm the one in the business suit) for your review…"

I was interviewed by the HR Director and then invited to interview with the President of the company. For the next step I was flown to the headquarters in Philadelphia to interview with the Senior Vice President who was in charge of the subsidiary, plus a few other top executives. Two months later when I started the job, I learned that the President, my boss, had a great sense of humor. He told me when he saw the photo and what I had written he told his HR Director, "Get me this guy!" THANKS MOM!

So it's January of 1992 and I'm the head of marketing and sales for Encore Service Systems, a company with $40 million per year in sales from providing A/C and appliance repair on a service contract basis. Encore was owned by ARA Services, the giant food services company. I reported directly to the President of Encore with five employees reporting to me. My salary was $50,000 per year and the workplace atmosphere was perfect – no jeans, but dress slacks and silk or cotton collared shirts. It was also a real 9 to 5 workday. At 5:01 p.m. the place was a ghost town.

If you've been paying attention up to now you would think this job ended my, "I don't know what I want to be when I grow up" part of my life, having found a good paying job with benefits, and security. It was also an exciting for-real marketing challenge to help grow the business, a very well established business with a large customer base. I rented my own apartment and my Dad signed for a used car with my agreement to pay the payments. I could breathe a little bit and the fresh air felt great! The storm had passed! Or was this just the calm within the eye of a hurricane?

Encore had been founded in 1973. In 1979 the founder sold out to ARA Services (now ARAMARK) and they kept him on as the subsidiary President. As long as he "made his numbers" each year the headquarters ostensibly let him have full control of the business. He told me only one year had they not met their numbers and the "suits" descended to spend a week auditing everything they could find to audit. There were seven other department heads like me who reported directly to the President and his Vice President. Most of the department heads and many employees had been with the company since the early days and they really were all like family. I learned that my predecessor had been fired about a year and half before basically because he had grown too big for his britches. The position was vacant and the woman who was to become my assistant and the three salesmen really did an okay job doing their jobs without a direct boss. But ARA had insisted the job vacancy be filled and they insisted it be filled with an MBA. From the first day I started work at Encore there was a chill in the air with some of my peers. I had no clue at the time but they suspected I was recruited to be a spy for headquarters! After about six months there was a typical visit from the ARA Senior VP and three of his staff. Fifteen of us were sitting in the President's office and after 45 minutes of discussion with other department heads the Senior VP asked, "So Jeff, how's the marketing and sales department?" You could hear a pin drop as my peers and boss held their breath awaiting my report. "Great!" I answered and I added a few details. All of them exhaled a sigh of relief at the same time. Too funny.

For about eight months I really tried to do my job. I was all gung-ho with "let's go get more business!" only to find that political infighting was actually sabotaging my efforts. I started to not know what I should do with my 8 hour day. Encore was a "mature" business before I got there so business remained at a fairly constant level without much effort or cost. The only thing potential customers wanted to know was if we could beat the price of our two main competitors in the area. Our pricing was in the hands of the accounting department head, and he didn't like me from our first meeting. I had a discussion about the pricing issue with the President and he said, "So you feel like your hands are tied behind your back?" and when I said "yes" he nodded his head but did not respond.

Shortly afterwards it was announced that ARA was selling Encore. I have no idea why, except it really was a relatively small subsidiary and it didn't fit well with their other businesses which were all food businesses. Also I had learned that over many years the President of Encore and his boss, the Senior VP at ARA, had exchanged more than one "fuck you". Before the announcement I felt the daily chill at work. Now it was frostbite. I believe that many of my co-workers believed I had some role in selling them out. Walking in their moccasins for a moment, it really made sense. Headquarters certainly could have worked a deal with me to provide an inside view in return for job security after a sale, maybe some other job within their huge company. I wished my co-workers only knew how grateful I was for a steady job and paycheck.

In hindsight I wished ARA *had* offered me a spy deal!

007 MBA!!!

Chapter 6
And One More Angel

"Only the most foolish of mice
would hide in a cat's ear.
But, only the wisest of cats
would think to look there!"
Buddhist proverb

You can't go looking for Angels because they are hiding, in plain sight. They find you at the right time and they have the right gift or message for you. An Angel will change your life, whether you like it or not!

"Sometimes even the flight of an angel
hits turbulence."
Astrid Alauda

And then there was Susan. It was October 1992 and I was having dinner at Wilt Chamberlain's restaurant in Boca with my Daughter, now 8 years old. The restaurant was basketball themed (of course) with lots of arcade games for the kids and even a mini basketball court. I sat at a table while my Daughter went off to play games and I looked at the menu. When I looked up from the menu, an Asian-American woman two tables away did the same thing, looking up from her menu directly at me. I could barely hear her say to me (very noisy restaurant), "What is good here?" I moved to her table and asked to sit down. She said "yes" and we introduced ourselves. Moments later my Daughter came to get more game tokens and at the same time another girl about the same age as my Daughter came to Susan's side, obviously her Daughter. We had a great time that night, got together for a lunch date a few days later, and the rest as they say was "history".

My depression was in high gear and I was smoking a lot of marijuana. Uncertainty at work had me not knowing if each day I showed up at work would be my last day. A relationship was the last thing I needed at the moment, but, "just say 'no'" never applied to women in my life.

One day at Susan's apartment she brought out an instruction book of Origami. I had done a little Origami as a kid and here was an activity we could do together. There is one particular flower called an Iris that had me captivated. With Origami as with most things in life, the more you repeat and practice the better you get. To me it seemed like each flower I made got a little better.

A huge part of success with hand-crafting, sports, and playing musical instruments is called "finger memory". My fingers adapted to the craft. I have great hands!

Susan showed me a foldout map of Seoul, South Korea. The outer card, front and back was postcard sized with photographs of the Seoul Hilton and the city of Seoul. Inside, like a sandwich, was a folded map of the city. I watched her open and close it, open and close it and was mesmerized by seeing the map unfold and fold, unfold and fold all by itself. She said, "I've had this for years. Somebody should make a business out of it." She added, "We should get one of the machines that make these!" I asked, "Do you know that it's done by machine? I'm guessing it is workers in Asia who fold them by hand."

My relationship with Susan was very stormy. In the course of five months I think we broke up six times and made up five times. One of those times was January 2, 1993. I was back at my apartment at about 10:00 p.m. with my passion ignited for getting back together with her, as I looked at the foldout map. I took apart the outer card and as soon as I saw the inner folded map the "light bulb" went on. When folded, the map has a "V" shaped bottom just like the V shaped bottom of a heart. If a square or rectangle could be folded this way, I knew a heart shape could be folded in the same way too. For three hours, with scissors and razor knife in hand, I played with a few designs, sizes and many different papers.

At 1:00 a.m. January 3, 1993 my first heart shaped Origami foldout greeting card was created, inspired from passion.

It worked! Susan loved the heart as did everyone who saw the few prototypes I had made. I received more than a few "you should be in the card business" comments and I certainly agreed. Susan and I lasted a few more weeks but our stormy relationship ended. And it also turned out that working for Encore had been just the eye of the hurricane and the back wall of the eye was now upon me.

The President of Encore had told me that, in a one on one meeting with the President and CEO of ARA, he was promised that he could put together a deal to match whatever offer ARA received for Encore, so he could buy back his company. I was somewhat comforted by this knowledge but still didn't know what that meant for my own future. I was not having good days at work. One Thursday the HR director told me to go home and take a long weekend to see if I could readjust my attitude. Friday I smoked marijuana, starting with breakfast, and in the early afternoon got a call from the HR director demanding I immediately go for drug testing or be fired. This was the early days of drug in the workplace policies and just a few months before I was responsible for reading out loud the newly instated policy to my department employees. But even in my smoky haze I knew there was something wrong with being called at home. The policy had "workplace" in its title and I was at home on an approved day off. I complied and tested positive (no surprise there).

I was fired. If the HR Director had nabbed me Monday morning at work the results would have been the same.

Two weeks later I learned that ARA had sold Encore to our major local competitor and the President was **not** given a chance to buy back his company.

Jobless again, no girlfriend, no money, and rent due in a few weeks along with a car payment. My familiarity with the panic of having no income came back in an instant. It had been a relatively nice year and a quarter. At least I had covered my rent, car payment, and partial child support too. But it was over. The back wall of the eye of the hurricane had hit me with full force, leaving me with nothing…

except an Origami heart shaped foldout card!

Was Susan sent to me?

Jay delivered a cocktail napkin rose and lifetime friendship. Sally delivered Prozac with her assurance of a better future. Susan delivered Origami cards & flowers, with passion.

My three Angels delivered, but I *still* didn't know what I wanted to be when I grew up!

Chapter 7
Down for the count

"The only thing worse than losing one's mind…
…is finding it!"
Me

Those of you who have experienced depression understand. Those of you who have not experienced depression are very fortunate, and don't understand. My Dad was a simple man and he didn't understand. He said, "Just put a smile on your face." So, I was depressed *and* smiling! Genetically I get my depression from my Mom's side of our family, but that's where I also get my creativity. Many creative people experience depression. Many creative people believe you can't have one without the other. I disagree. I'm more creative without depression.

"Cause suicide is painless.
It brings on many changes.
And I can take or leave it if I please.
…and you can do the same thing if you please."
Refrain from lyrics (Michael Altman) of M.A.S.H.
movie and TV show

March 16, 1993. My plan was somehow to use a vacuum cleaner hose and sit myself in my car inhaling fumes. I never worked out the details. I wrote a letter to my almost 9 year old Daughter and put it with a few other things in a manila envelope. I put one of my Origami flowers in there too. I proceeded to smoke great quantities of marijuana and got started on a bottle of 15 year old Scotch.

Very painful. Very, very painful. Very, very, very painful. To those of you who experience depression, you know what I've experienced. I characterize it as walking into a very dark forest. It is amazing that I kept walking, came out the other side and now can write about it. Many people walk into this same dark forest. Most don't make it out.

I drove to the beach after dark and walked on the sand about a mile to a prominent rock formation jutting into the ocean. It was my favorite spot and I had sat there often. I had a lot of beach time in Florida so the beach was where I chose to say "goodbye". That night was perfect for the scene, windy and misty, ocean with a good chop. There I was, on my rock saying my goodbyes, drinking Scotch.

I drove back to my apartment, thought about what I was planning to do next, and broke down. I was kneeling on the floor with my head to the floor, crying. I looked over at the manila envelope I was leaving behind. The bright yellow Origami flowers were sticking out, and I thought,

> ***"If my fingers can make something that beautiful,
> then there's gotta be a place for me in this world."***

I had hit bottom.

I woke up the next day (still on the floor) and called my Psychologist (I had started seeing her in January) for an emergency appointment. March 17, 1993 I'm sitting in my Psychologist's office telling her about yesterday and last night. I expressed to her that as I sat on my rock I just wanted to end the emotional pain I had experienced for too many years and now it was the worst ever. I told her, "I didn't feel ANYTHING last night, no feeling or connection to remorse and no emotion for ending my life." She replied, "Did you ever think it might be the drugs?" I sorta laughed to myself because no, until that moment I had never considered that pot was a problem and not a solution. She asked if I had ever heard of NA, Narcotics Anonymous and I said "no" but knew it had to be like AA which I only knew existed. She suggested I go to a meeting, challenging me to go just once to see what I thought of it. I respond well to being challenged!

Back at my apartment I opened up a phone book and dialed an NA number and left my number on a message machine. I had no idea what it was about, but figured maybe it's a group that meets once per month. My phone rang and after a little chat with the volunteer I asked, "When is the next meeting?" and he said, "Tonight" and I echoed, "Tonight?" Wow, that kinda meant I had to go…tonight.

The meeting was in a classroom at a local Jewish Temple. There were about 35 people. The speaker was a "kid", piercings and weird hair, and then he started talking. His story sounded a lot like mine! He talked about his feelings of just not fitting in with his family, job, and society.

NA meetings became an important, very important part of my life from 1993 through 1997ish. For many days and nights each week I sought out NA meetings. In one sense I felt out of place. I understand in California they have Marijuana Anonymous for us potheads. California, of course! I met a few addicts with similar pot problems, but for the most part this was a hardcore crowd – never met a drug they didn't try at least twice, three times if the first two didn't kill them. I felt more fortunate than most and heard stories that made my own life seem like simply a mere manageable mess. NA meetings were also a form of walk-in counseling for me, a place where I could openly talk about anything. It gave me a safe place to go with meetings available all over South Florida every day and night. I got hooked on the free coffee. I stopped smoking.

Each of our bodies is different. In my body, marijuana triggers depression. Alcohol is no big deal for me, and even though I've written about drinking 15 year old Scotch, my norm is just a beer every now and then, and I rarely go on to a second beer. I feel an alcoholic's recovery challenge is greater than that of a drug addict because alcohol is everywhere, and an accepted part of our society.

During this time period I read a lot of self-help, spiritual, and inspiring books. I even got a hand-typed response back from a letter I sent to Og Mandino where I referred to his concept of a "ragpicker." He used the term ragpicker to mean someone who rescues people who ended up in life's refuse pile, people who just need a little help at the right time and place. **I had put myself in life's refuse pile.** Og apologized for not having any "ragpicker" contacts for me, but the fact that he responded at all gave me a little lift.

Was Jay my "ragpicker"?

"Suicide is a permanent solution to a temporary problem". That strikes my sense of logic. What if my problems really were temporary??? I read an interesting comment by an Australian who said he felt their suicide rate was lower since the country started a lottery, because with a lottery ticket in your pocket you want to hang around *at least* for the next drawing! Then, when you don't win, you buy a ticket for next week's lottery.   I can relate to this. I bought a lottery ticket each week. Hope in weekly dosages. No matter what one's circumstances, we can't give up hope.

Two frogs jumping around a barn jump into a pail of milk and can't get out. After a half hour of trying, one frog succumbs to the inevitable, slides under the surface and drowns. The second frog keeps on kicking. The milk turns to cream, then to butter and now the frog can get a foothold and jumps out to safety. Moral of the story?

When you're in over your head just keep on kicking!

I asked my Psychologist, "Will I ever be happy?" She pondered, not answering for quite a few seconds, and then said, "Yes". I responded, "I don't think so, but I'd settle just for the absence of pain." I kept on kicking, and now many years later, it turns out that… she was right!

I was on Prozac from May of 1990 when Sally first put one in my mouth, to 1998 when my new family doctor was discussing my history with Prozac. He said, "Everybody deserves a chance to be off anti-depressants. I go by a two strike rule. You go off it once. If you find you need it, you're back on it. Then you try to go off it again. If you have to go back on it again, then you're on it for life."

I stopped taking Prozac and over the next few weeks felt…no difference, no difference at all. I think the absence of pot and the hardware rewiring of being on Prozac, plus aging some years, gave me the ability to handle whatever residual depression I experienced.

On March 17, 1993 I began to walk *OUT* of the dark forest.

GENTLEMEN, I ASK YOU, WHAT IS ART?
ART IS A CONTRACT BETWEEN ARTIST AND PARTICIPANT IN WHICH THE PARTICIPANT'S STATE OF EMOTION HAS BEEN BRIEFLY ALTERED.
AUGH!
THUS, IN ONE FLEETING MOMENT ART HAS BEEN CREATED.
AND ANOTHER SOUL HAS BEEN TOUCHED BY MY INSPIRATION.
THAT'S WHY I WAS GIVEN CLAWS...
... TO MAKE THEM SCREAM, TO MAKE THEM CRY, TO REMIND THEM THEY'RE ALIVE.
HE'S A GENIUS.
HE'S JUST A CRAB WITH GOOD MARKETING.
http://www.slagoon.com

Part 2
I'm just a crab with good marketing

I'm sure you have your own favorite cartoon, one that says "that's me!" to you. This one is mine. I have a framed, autographed, color print in my office. I'd have the original if it was available, but somebody else already purchased it. I guess I'm not the only "crab with good marketing"!

Sherman's Lagoon
By Jim Toomey
© 1999 Jim Toomey
Used with permission from the artist

Chapter 8
No, I'm NOT a team player

*"There are two ways to get to the top of an oak tree.
You can climb it or you can sit on an acorn and wait!"*
Zig Ziglar

You know when you're interviewing for a great job and
your potential boss asks you, "Are you a team player?"
What's your only answer? "YEAH, HELL YEAH!"
Well, I'm NOT a team player. It took me fifteen years in
the working world to realize I'm not a team player and
don't work well as an employee. If I were a team player on
a football team I'd be a wide receiver. Don't invite me into
the huddle. I'll go "long" every time. I'll be open half the
time. When you throw it to me I'll catch it half the time.
Don't invite me into the huddle. Oh, and one more thing –
don't invite me into the huddle.

"I did it my way."
From the song "My Way"
Lyrics by Paul Anka
Popularized by Frank Sinatra

So my last attempt at a corporate career ended in February 1993. No job, so I had to move back to my parents' house. The rest of that year was dark, very dark as I began a very slow climb back up from my personal bottom.

I started grasping for any job, just as I had done before my job with Encore. Back to the classified ads and taking any sales job that held out promise. I lasted from two weeks to three months in these jobs, never making more than subsistence money. My list got longer. In 1993 and 1994 my jobs were selling knock-off merchandise, selling BBB memberships, selling employment ads, and last but not least, selling in home dog training service.

More "selling the sizzle."

My first post Encore job was a phone/fax operation that would do fax-blasts of merchandise almost all of which was knock-off logo merchandise. I decided to use their fax to contact seven attorneys with my case for a wrongful termination suit against Encore. One of the seven responded and we proceeded with a lawsuit. When I ended my short employment with the fax-blast operation I phoned one of the trademarked shirt companies and provided info as to what was going on, and they paid me $500 for the info. I didn't like being a snitch, but I needed the $500.

My next job was a short stint selling memberships for the local Better Business Bureau. Their ad in the paper said $600 per week possible and leads provided. The job was onsite in their office, in a converted closet that held six of us, with desks and phones. We were actually hired by a company that was contracted by the BBB to do their sales. Their leads were the Yellow Pages. The pitch was to call up local companies, tell them there was an inquiry on their company but because they're not members all we could give out was public information, and then we would ask to come to their place of business immediately to sign them up with the BBB. If they said "yes", we would be in our car within minutes. I really can't figure the BBB because they only have "power" to resolve disputes involving members, and even then if a member doesn't want to resolve, nothing is resolved. It seems to be a self-serving organization to provide employment for its executives and employees. After two weeks of working in the closet I wondered, "Who do I call to complain about the BBB?"

My next job was with a rather sizeable and successful company that was doing employment advertising and hosting job fairs. I liked the owner and what the company was doing, but again my job was "smiling and dialing" telephone selling all day. I was at this job three months when my lawsuit was scheduled for a possible settlement. ARA settled for $40K in late 1993. My attorney got $15K and I got $25K. I gave my ex-Wife $5K to make up for a little back child support. I quit my job and moved into an apartment with a guy who was looking for a roommate.

Free at last?

Not quite.

While I was miserable, stumbling from job to job, at least I was keeping my head above water. I now felt it had all lead up to the point where my Origami heart-shaped card would be the "answer" to all my employment problems. It was time to set up my greeting card company.

It was like getting out of jail and being set free. I no longer would have to work for someone else, no more teams! I took my hand cut prototypes to a paper die cutter and we did a production run of about 25,000 cards in two pieces – outer card, heart shaped and die cut from glossy red card stock, and the inner paper heart printed with 13 different Valentine sayings, "You've Opened My Heart", etc. The inner heart shape was die cut from matte red paper and die scored for the hand folding yet to come.

I went to a custom PVC fabricator where we designed a heart shaped countertop greeting card display standing about two feet tall and on a swivel base so each side could be loaded with five different cards. The cards and display looked great! This was my very first glimpse, at age 39, of my own creative design talents and I liked the results. I also liked the process of mass creating a product. Figuring out how to do something can be intellectually very stimulating and satisfying when the results come out as expected or, even better than expected. This was my first glimpse at what I wanted to be when I grew up!

I named the company Lotus Entertain You, Inc. and incorporated in the State of Florida in April 1994. I cloned the name from a successful Chicago restaurateur whose company is Lettuce Entertain You Enterprises.
I thought the name was cute as a lotus flower represents "unfolding" or blossoming in Eastern cultures and also reflects the Eastern origins of the art of Origami.

When I had hand folded and glued enough of the initial production it was time for the grand unveiling! So far every family member or friend who saw my heart shaped fold out cards absolutely loved them and said, "You should be in the card business!" I had no focus group before going to production. I didn't need anyone else's opinion to tell me that my cards were cute and salable, but I hadn't yet sold one card. There was a weekly Thursday night sunset celebration at a local marina where about 25 arts and crafts vendors set up for a mini-show. I set up my greeting cards with a sign saying "$3 each, 2 for $5". A woman walked by, stopped, picked up and opened a few cards, picked out two and gave me a $5 bill. My heart was pounding so hard I thought people could see it beating through my clothes. Somebody BOUGHT my cards, and she was NOT a friend or family! I was in business!!!

I knew what I wanted to be when I grew up!

I was doing what I loved, but if the money was following, it was so far behind me that I still couldn't even see it with a telescope! If this were what I wanted to be when I grew up then I needed to sell lots of greeting cards, maybe 250,000 per year at a minimum, to make a fulltime living.

But I didn't have to be a team player!

As the settlement money went mostly into my inventory of cards and displays, I found myself needing a job again. I found my very last commissioned sales job, selling in-home dog training. This was actually on the up and up, but maybe like the adjustable bed business, it was selling an overpriced service to people who thought a dog trainer would train their dog. They learned as they went through the sessions with the trainer, that it was more about training the human than about training the dog, and the most essential ingredient is practice. Practice, practice, practice.

Woof! NOT what I wanted to be when I grew up!

Chapter 9
DWIT
in a Limo

"You're gonna have to serve somebody."
From the song "Gotta Serve Somebody"
By Bob Dylan

I have two other hobbies. One is sleeping with a roof over my head, and the other is eating at least twice per day. Sometimes ya just gotta do what ya gotta do. But many limo jobs were on the clock, getting paid for wait time. Getting paid to just sit in a nice Lincoln Town Car or stretch limousine, read a book, snooze, or work on my business is maybe the best job description there can be. One night, *I got paid* to watch naked women dance!

"Service makes men competent"
Lyman Abbott

DWIT – Do Whatever It Takes

"Whatever" has no definition and means different things to different people, especially those heading up the path of an entrepreneur. Almost every success story has some report of sacrifice, usually above and beyond the call of duty. Entrepreneurial sacrifice means giving up time, energy and money that might be spent elsewhere to now focus on your business. What are you willing to give up? What are you willing to do to see your dreams come true?

Will YOU do whatever it takes?

Part of my DWIT was my decision to drive for a limo company while ramping up Lotus EntertainYou. I had driven for a few months during the winter of 1990 so I knew the gig. I figured I could stick it out six months by which time my greeting card business would be self-sustaining. Six months turned out to be five years! Had I known in advance that it would be five years I might not have cleared the launch pad. Six months of doing anything is doable. But five years? Actually it was five rather okay years, except for when I had to wake up at 3:00 a.m. to go to the Miami airport for 5:00 a.m. pickups!

In August 1994 my ex-Wife and I had dated and decided to get back together again. We had been apart six years but had a common focus on our Daughter. I moved into their apartment and confused the heck out of our 10 year old Daughter. Her first question was, "So why did you guys get divorced?" We had no good answer.

I began driving. Working for a limo company means airport work, lots of airports. I used to joke with drivers that I was going to start Airports Anonymous – "Do you wake up at 2:00 a.m. with an urge to drive to the nearest airport? Well just call us at Airports Anonymous…" South Florida has three major airports, West Palm Beach, Fort Lauderdale, and Miami plus several executive airports scattered about. While our clientele lived mostly in Palm Beach County, all the airports were used. One day I did a pickup or dropoff at four different airports!

On weekend nights (weekends often are sacrificed for DWIT) when you might be driving a stretch limousine, you are NOT part of the party. Basically there are two types of drivers, lifers and those just passing through. I found I liked most of the drivers better than the people I'd met in the business world. It's an honest day's work for about $100 net, maybe $125 average. I have lots of stories of my own and lots of stories shared by other drivers. The next time you're at a sporting event or concert look at all the limo drivers hanging out by their cars – they're on the clock **getting paid to BS with each other!**

Lotus Entertain You was a Valentine's Day card product. The task was to get them out in stores during the first two weeks of January each year. The first year I put displays in about 85 gift stores on consignment and they sold well in many locations. Several problems – some stores went out of business before I was able to collect and get back my display. Plus, there just isn't much money in a greeting card that sells once per year. My best store was a unique gift store in Mizner Park in Boca Raton, a very high traffic upscale shopping center. This store sold about 300 of our cards each year, $200 revenue for me. I would stand to the side in the store to watch people pick up a card and play with it, opening and closing, opening and closing, and then buy it! The Origami fold-out card has a hypnotizing motion as you open it and close it, open it and close it. I needed about 199 stores like this one to make a go of the greeting card business! So that became my task, to find 199 stores that would sell like my best one. The stores are out there and it's really not a challenge to find them. The challenge was to get them to buy my cards.

In 1995 and again in 1996 I attended the Greeting Card Association awards dinner in NYC where the main event is the awarding of the "Louie" for best greeting cards. I had entered my cards into the Valentine's Day category. It's a judged contest. I won a Louie Award both years and have photos on our website of the 1st year with Jerry Stiller presenting me the award and for the 2nd year, Steve Allen. I got some good local press coverage. Yes, I won the awards, but it was still my job to take out the trash!

While local sales were okay, or at least a confirmation that some people would buy our cards, national distribution was elusive. Through a contact of my friend Jay, my cards and display were shown to a product distributor who did a lot of business with K-Mart. The report from this contact was that in his 15 years of dealing with this distributor he had never seen a reaction like the one he got from our cards!

Shortly afterwards I received a phone call from the distributor asking if I could handle 500,000 cards! Of course I said "yes" and then when I hung up the phone I wondered just how was I going handle 500,000 cards?

Remember, Susan thought the foldout map was machine folded and I thought they would be die cut and die scored and then hand folded. I saw a few more of these maps in local gift shops with maps of their local area and of course the name of the printer was on them. Unbelievable - the map business was in Boca Raton! Jay and I visited and saw a very nice niche business. It was owned by an elderly man and he had one ancient automated folding machine. Even the patent was expired! I never saw it working but it looked cool, a real clankety-clank type of machine with lots of moving parts. The owner liked my heart shaped card and he gave us a price quote to fold and glue them. His customers were mostly towns and cities who wanted a promotional map to sell in local stores. The printing was printed by a standard printer. Then the job was taken to a die cutter. Lastly, he and a worker cranked up the machine to do the folding, followed by hand gluing.

I made inquiries about getting the cards made in China and got a price quote – 10 cents each for the complete finished product, including everything but shipping. It was do-able! Within two weeks we got bad news from the distributor. Apparently it was the jewelry buyer of K-Mart who wanted our cards for counter-top display for Valentine's Day, but K-Mart's greeting card buyer killed the deal. The only cards in K-Mart were made by American Greetings Co.

Nationally the greeting card market is fairly closed out by Hallmark, American Greetings and a few second tier companies. Hallmark had returned my solicitation, unopened, with a nice note explaining that they have hundreds of full time card designers on staff, so they don't look at anything from the outside.

Meanwhile I got articles published in local papers about winning the Louie Awards! I laminated copies of stories, which included photos of me with Jerry Stiller and Steve Allen, and then I put them in the magazine pocket facing the passengers in the back seat of my Town Car.

South Florida is a place where a lot of wealthy people live, at least part of the year. It's also where every celebrity, sports star, or politician visits sooner or later. My stories could fill a book by themselves. Many times my articles in the magazine pocket triggered an, "is this you?" opener to a conversation. Many times, if not most times, the people in my back seat were successful business people. I enjoy business discussions, especially entrepreneurial business discussions. I never miss a chance to chat about my business and ask you questions about yours. There are hundreds of wealthy communities in South Florida. We regularly serviced clients in Admiral's Cove and Frenchman's Creek in Palm Beach County, as well as the island of Palm Beach where almost every resident is a "captain" of industry. The Four Seasons and Ritz Carlton hotels are also both on the beach in Palm Beach County.

With all passengers in my car I was always courteous and conscious of the concept of "opening the door" (literally and figuratively). If a customer in my back seat opened up the conversation then I joined in and carried my part of the conversation, but I never initiated the conversations.
I had a unique opportunity to ask many successful people, "What do you do?" and, "Do you like what you do?"

One conversation, for example, was with a man I drove from the airport to his nice home in Boca Raton. We struck up a conversation and he told me he had been 40 years in the logo watch business. He said his two Sons were in the business with him. I asked a question you should ask EVERY successful person when you can, "If you had to do it over again, would you?" to which he responded, "NO, I've spent the past 25 years being a bill collector, trying to get my money." I remember his story when I describe JustPaperRoses.com as "credit card enabled". I have NO receivables. I'm never chasing a customer for money or even waiting for a check to clear.

I drove Steve Forbes when he was running for President. I asked him for an explanation of his proposal for a flat tax and we had a great conversation. He saw my articles and I gave him one of my heart shaped card. I asked him, "When you are in the White House, can I create a fold out card with the Presidential seal?" He answered "yes"!

He ~~bought~~ got my vote!

My list of "names" is long and ranges from quarterback
Jim Kelly to Reverend Robert Schuller, with stops in
between for Rosemary Kennedy, the Sultan of Brunei, and
Prince Alwaleed Bin Talal Alsaud of Saudi Arabia.
Al Roker was fun and Diane Sawyer was "all business".
Dan Quail wasn't sure where he was, and Mark Hamill
carried his own backpack. I should have kept a diary!

My favorite day and a half was in a Town Car with
Senator Bill Bradley after he had retired and written a
book. I didn't need to ask him, "What do you do?"
He was on a book signing tour, speaking in a book store
Sunday evening in Boca Raton, and another Monday night
in Coral Gables in the Miami area. Sunday afternoon and
all day Monday we went from radio station to radio station
where he was an interviewed guest. In between interviews
we would stop in book stores unannounced and he would
go in to sign a bunch of his books. It was just me and him
in the car and I ate lunch with him too. Turns out he is a
Wendy's fan! My 2cents with him was to suggest that
small businesses should get the first $100K revenue each
year tax free, and if a business is below $100K then
paperwork free too. He agreed! Now that I've experienced
my business, I'll raise that number to $1M.

Entrepreneurs are the lifeblood of our economy and we
should be helping them get off the ground. Why do we
want to tax them when they are just getting started?

To slow them down ???

From 1994 through 1998 I kept trying to be in the card business, creating a few different shapes of foldouts based on the same Origami map fold – sports balls mostly but also a variety of company logos. I could take most logos and do some sort of fold out card based on the shape. I began sending unsolicited samples to businesses. It has taken me fifteen years to finally stop sending unsolicited samples of my products. The short story is that for the fifteen years of doing this I've received zilch, nothing. I believe it's very subtle psychology of the sale. When someone is on the search for something, they are receptive to many things they find for possible purchase. When someone receives a sample unsolicited, the "wall of negativity" gets raised. Also my samples to corporations are always to a marketing person who usually operates from the fear of making a mistake rather than from the chance of hitting a home run. My fold-out card products with logos are called advertising specialties. A man in the specialties business once told me, "My clients every year ask me, 'what is new and different?' and then they buy coffee mugs, baseball caps, t-shirts, calendars and pens."

By the time the business morphed into JustPaperRoses.com it had already become evident I was going nowhere in the card business. I STILL have heart shaped cut outs in my garage, awaiting assembly. For several years annually I donated cards for a Valentine's Day fundraiser for the American Heart Association, but the Origami greeting card business folded. (Sorry, I couldn't resist the pun.)

Another great limo story is one where I was paid on the clock 8 hours and did nothing. I was now driving for a small private company with 2 stretches and 3 Town Cars. One of their best accounts was the Slim-Fast company. Danny Abraham, the creator of Slim-Fast had moved his company to West Palm Beach and we drove his employees to and from airports, as well as doing some personal driving for him and his family. We didn't do security work, but the owner of the limo company was a disabled Philadelphia police officer so we all checked out squeaky clean when it came to driving high profile clients.

One night I was assigned to be just an extra Town Car in case it was needed, to meet the Slim-Fast jet at the West Palm Beach airport when it landed from Israel with Mr. Abraham and his Wife, Mr. Shimon Peres and his Wife, and two security agents on board. There was to be a small motorcade from the airport to Mr. Abraham's residence in Palm Beach with a Presidential bullet-proof limo and security cars driven by our Secret Service. Mr. Abraham is philanthropic and personally active in seeking an Israeli/Palestinian solution. Upon his invitation, Shimon Peres was speaking in Palm Beach. The plane was due in about 11 p.m. I arrived at the private aviation side of the West Palm Beach airport at 6 p.m., the first one there.

Shortly after I arrived, the Palm Beach Sheriffs showed up with the bomb sniffing dog. One officer told me to stand away from my car as he circled the car once with his dog. The dog sat (called "spotting") and looked at my driver's door. The officer and dog circled the car once again and the dog "spotted" again. The officer looked at me and I instinctively raised my hands in surrender! He asked if he could inspect my car. He did, of course finding nothing, and then suggested that the nitrates in our car cleaning solutions might be what his dog had smelled.

Then the Palm Beach SWAT arrived, followed by the U.S. Secret Service and finally the Israeli Shin-Bet (their Secret Service) complete with rifles slung across their backs. I radio'd my boss:

> "There are now 7 vehicles and 19 people on the ground.
> I AM THE ONLY ONE WITHOUT A GUN!
> You don't pay me enough for this!!!"

The Secret Service had pulled up a bullet-proof Presidential limo, an old Lincoln Continental. Security vehicles were lined up for the motorcade with the limo in the middle. About 10:30 p.m., a Jet Aviation employee pulled up Danny Abraham's bright red BMW convertible and parked it at the end of the line of vehicles. I guess he only knew that the Slim-Fast jet was landing and for him it was just business as usual? How could he have missed the 18 guys with guns??? One of the Secret Service agents turned to me and asked, "Whose car is that?" and I responded, "That's Mr. Abraham's car. He likes to drive himself and will probably put Mr. Peres and his Wife in the back seat, put down the top and give them his own guided tour of Palm Beach!" The agent didn't laugh. He ordered the employee to put the car back in the parking lot.

The plane was late and at about midnight I got a call from my boss saying Mr. Abraham had called him directly from the plane to tell him wheels would be down at 12:15 a.m. I walked over to the Secret Service agents and said, "Wheels down in 15 minutes" and the same agent as before now glared at me and asked, "How do YOU know?"

The plane landed and the procession made it to the residence without a shot fired, although I think the Secret Service agents wanted to pop me just for fun! My lesson from that night was that people who carry guns as part of their job description leave their sense of humor at home!

I opened this chapter mentioning naked women, so I have to tell you one more limo story. We rarely did limo work for the hard party crowd. Our clientele were the wealthier people in South Florida and many limo gigs were simply taking two or three couples out to dinner, sporting event, concert or social party, waiting for them and then returning. One night I was assigned a bachelor party. The client was a man in his 30s who owned a drywall contracting business, was getting married, and he knew the owner of the limo company so we booked this bachelor party. The six guys giving him the party were his employees. I pulled up to the Groom's townhouse and out stroll seven "cowboys" each more handsome than next and a few were obviously gym rats. I thought to myself, "Oh no, I'm in for a rough and long night." A limo driver's responsibility is to keep the car clean, immaculate. Every time the clients leave the car the driver cleans up the passenger area. When clients come back to the car it's supposed to look just like when they started out for the evening. The trunk has cleaning supplies and backup glassware too. Also, the gig ends when the client says it ends, so I thought I'd be seeing sunrise with these cowboys!

They got in the car and the first thing one of them said to one guy was, "If you light up a cigarette we're throwing you out the window!" Bingo! That was a relief for me to hear, for while there were NO SMOKING signs in the back, when clients raised the privacy screen many times the signs were ignored. They kept the privacy screen down and when I started to drive I saw in my rear view mirror that they were popping open cans of beer they brought with them. I offered, "You're welcome to use the glassware" and the Groom responded, "No, we'll just drink from the cans". Bingo again! No glassware to clean all night long! The itinerary was bar hopping to 5 or 6 nude bars – South Florida's finest. At the first stop the guys gathered their cans and tossed those into a trash can on their way into the club. Bingo yet again! No trash for me to clean up! At the second club the Groom asked me, "Why don't you park the limo and come in with us?" Bingo again? As a limo driver I wasn't supposed to leave the car unattended, so I had to ponder my decision for at least 3 seconds…and there I was, inside the club, watching naked women dance, while getting paid $25 per hour on the clock!!! Bless America!!!

I returned the party to the townhouse at about 2:00 a.m., and when I checked the limo passenger area it was immaculate, just like when I arrived. GREAT gig!

Do Whatever It Takes. My five years of driving limos was an important part of my business startup, but also a part I wouldn't want to do over again. I kept motivated by focusing on my vision of my greeting card business becoming full time, but also grew comfortable with the vision of being a driver the rest of my life if my business never lifted off the launching pad. It was a very humbling experience. I am an Ivy League engineering graduate with an MBA from one of the best business schools in the country, and here I was hanging out in airports with one of those greeter signs, carrying luggage for clients too. But, it was also five years of fresh air, both literally because the job is out and about, and also because I was providing a good service for clients, getting paid to do so.

"You're gonna have to serve somebody."

What is YOUR DWIT? What would you do to get to where you want to be? Can you accept where you are now? Can you enjoy your journey and its hardships while staying true to your vision? Can you be okay with the possibility of your dreams never coming true, while at the same time working as if the outcome were guaranteed?

Chapter 10
The Birth of JustPaperRoses

*"Every act of creation is first of all
an act of destruction."*
Pablo Picasso

And there goes my hobby! I don't know exactly when it happened, but at some point my hobby of Origami wasn't fun anymore, or maybe more accurately it's not what I was doing in my spare time. And there goes my spare time too, as I now had a baby business that needed all my attention!

*"Imagination was given to man to compensate him for
what he is not.
A sense of humor was provided to console him for
what he is!"*
Horace Walpole

For two weeks during the summer of 1999 I was an art instructor at a local art camp for kids age 5 through 12. I was the Origami teacher. It was a real busy day of six different age group classes for an hour each. There were also about ten other instructors teaching their art or craft. You could feel the creativity in the air. The non-stop screaming voices of the kids were in the air too!

I enjoy teaching and I enjoy kids but I had never taught a structured class for kids before. I thought that by the end of two weeks I would lead them up to being able to make my Origami Orchids (photo on back cover – in my pocket). WRONG. Origami can get complicated fairly quick, so one basic principal of Origami is "neatness counts". Every fold amplifies the imprecision of the fold before it, so it's easy to end up with a folded mess. I quickly learned that most of the age 5 through 8 year olds won't be able to fold a piece of paper neatly in half. The 9 through 12 year olds were better to varying degrees. So I found some books with beginner Origami models that didn't require too many folds, but ended up with simple animal, birds, or other shapes, which could be colored with crayons too.

The kids liked and had fun with everything we did.

One of the reasons Origami is popular with children in Eastern countries is because all it requires is a discarded newspaper to have some fun. One of the more amazing "finds" I saw in a beginner Origami book was a "game" of stacking. So simple. Cut an 8.5 x 11 inch card stock into 5 strips, 8.5 x 2. Bend them in the middle to form an open triangle. These strips can now be set on the floor or table standing sideways. Hand a whole bunch of them to kids and announce a contest to see who can build the highest tower in two categories – single strip on each level, and free formed using a base as large as you wish. Wow, the kids got hooked on this stacking game! In our second week it got me *off* the hook because I was running out of Origami animals and shapes to teach. The kids loved it and some of the older kids built stacks to the ceiling!

Then, I showed the kids how to twirl a napkin around their fingers to make a paper napkin rose (photo on back cover). This too excited the kids almost as much as the stacking game, because it was a flower they could make for Mommy or Daddy. At the time I had been making my Origami Orchids with a very nice art paper that has a pearled finish and a great texture – takes a great crease. As I was showing one of the kids how to make a napkin rose, I thought, (drum roll please…*this is* **"it"**…):

"Why don't I see if I can make an "upscale" cocktail napkin rose, using my nice art paper?"

That night the JustPaperRose was born, although not yet named as such. I created the blossom the same way as with a napkin, twirling a nice art paper around my fingers. But instead of using the rest of the paper as a stem and leaf the way it's done with a napkin, I used a standard floral wire, floral tape, and inserted a paper Origami leaf midway on the stem. I wish I had saved the first one.

I created my new paper roses with white, orange, and red pearled art paper and I put them on the website. They started to sell. A friend said, "Of course they are selling. Your Origami Orchids are beautiful, but a guy isn't sure his Wife will like them and he doesn't want to make a mistake. But roses are roses are roses." I don't remember if I knew the 1st Anniversary is traditionally the "paper" Anniversary or if a customer told me. It really doesn't matter how I knew, because I quickly became micro-focused on the niche for 1st "paper" Wedding Anniversary gifts.

In late 1999 a then soon to be defunct dot.com called me to ask if I could do something "signature" for them with my paper roses. I immediately thought "logo" and knew I could print their logo on our white pearled art paper and then make the paper rose. The first samples came out great and "POOF" I was now in the personalization business. I created samples printed with names, "1st Anniversary" and date, then spent the next two months redoing the website to now focus on personalized paper roses for the 1st "paper" Wedding Anniversary.

This was starting to be fun! I wasn't comfortable with a title of "artist" but maybe "crafter" was a better fit. I used COO – Chief Origami Officer or sometimes I was the CFO – Chief Folding Officer on my business cards, emails and letters. All I needed to do was increase the business to 20 times its current pace to approach a full time income!

Near the end of my limo driving gig I had met Mr. Bloch – no relation to me, and his name was with an "h" and mine is with a "k". I picked up a bunch of business people at the airport and drove them to his home in Frenchman's Creek. He was in the airport greeting them, in his wheelchair. I knew his personal assistant/driver and I saw and chatted with Mr. Bloch a few times that week when I was picking up or dropping off his guests. Mr. Bloch was ailing from a degenerative muscular disease. He would gradually lose control of his body and yes, he has passed away.

I now called his assistant to ask about Mr. Bloch and to see if he would be interested to see samples of my newly created paper roses. A year before, when Mr. Bloch had chatted with me, he told me he was in the industrial paper business and I had shown him and given him a few of my Origami heart cards. I was eager to show him what was new, as the business had quickly morphed from cards to paper roses. His assistant reported back that Mr. Bloch would love to see what I had. My samples were well received and I was invited to visit. He liked my stuff. His paper business had designed a new layered material for large envelopes and he excitedly showed me samples, wondering too if I could do something with his new paper.

Even though Mr. Bloch was ailing he demonstrated vigor and joy when he discussed his business. We sat at his kitchen table in his very nice home. It wasn't the biggest or the most expensive in the neighborhood, but in this neighborhood every house is amazing and expensive.

He called out to his Wife to "come take a look at these" and I almost shouted "NO!" Our average customer spends (today) $65 and I was sitting in a house looking at original art on the walls. I have no issue stating our paper roses, especially the way they looked back then, are not a high-end product. Plus it was not the Bloch's 1st "paper" Anniversary so she'd be viewing them out of context. His Wife came over to the table, quickly looked at the sample dozen, packaged beautifully in a clear long-stem rose box.

Her comment was "eh".

I thought I was there to ask to borrow $250K for the business. I made the request. Mr. Bloch responded, "I'm well beyond the age where return on investment means anything to me, and besides if I did invest it would be far more than $250K. What would you do with $5 million?" To which I answered, "With all due respect, I'd put $250K into the business, $4.75 million into T-bills, and probably go to the beach a lot!" With that we moved into his home office. Then I heard the classic line, "You don't need money, what you need is contacts!" and before I could say, "NO, really, I could use some money" he had his assistant get out his phone book and his assistant started dialing. It was amazing how many people took his call, even when the receptionist first said, "I think he's busy but I'll see." Mr. Bloch ended our meeting by saying, "I won't give you $250,000 for your business, but I'd give you $1 million for your body." He was serious. Then he chuckled, smiled and added "I'd give you $1 million just for your dick!"

Now I admit to being guilty of overvaluing my, you know what, but it left me wondering if Mr. Bloch valued me at $1 million, why wasn't I valuing myself at $1 million too?

This was February, 2000. About a week later I was sitting in my home office when the phone rang and a man with a deep voice asked for "Jeff Block". When I said it was me, he replied, "This is Morry Weiss of American Greetings. Gil Bloch asked that I call you". Morry Weiss is the Chairman of American Greetings Company! I couldn't believe it, a Chairman of a $2 billion company telephoning me directly! It turns out Mr. Weiss has a winter home a few doors down from The Blochs and they had known each other for many years.

Mr. Weiss was more than cordial. He told me he doesn't make product decisions but referred me to the President of his Carlton Cards division (retail stores) and to the President of AmericanGreetings.com their website business. The website President basically said he couldn't really discount advertising space on the site because I'd be taking the space of a full paying customer. The rack rate cost of the space was way over my head. The retail store President took a few more steps. We were discussing our RealMoneyTree for sale in their stores. I thought then, as I do at this very moment, that the RealMoneyTree has potential as the next "Pet Rock". It's a JustPaperRose made from a real $1 bill, "planted" in a small terra cotta pot. We even include two packets of "money tree seeds" (3 pennies) with instructions to "grow your own"!

After the store President told me that she really liked the product she went on, "But I have to tell you, we buy at 40% of retail not 50%, you have to take returns, and we pay on 90 day terms." It was a "take it or leave it" offer and I had to leave it. I'd have to spend my money to create inventory, ship it to their stores, hope it sells and then get paid 90 days later on what sold, with the rest returned. Basically, it's a consignment business model.

While nothing came to fruition with American Greetings it is still a great story. How many times will you get a direct personal phone call from the head of a major corporation? Also I think this experience quickly solidified my business model as direct-to-customer rather than wholesale-to-retail.

By April, 2000 it seemed appropriate to change our name from LotusEntertainYou.com. As a funny side note, a few years before I had received a "nastygram" from the lawyers for Lettuce Entertain You Enterprises. Actually it really was an okay letter asking for more information because they weren't sure there was a conflict, yet they did include a dozen examples of trademark infringement they had prosecuted in the past. I had created a football shaped schedule foldout for a local kid's football team and used it as a sample to solicit professional football teams and some colleges too. I believe that Lettuce Entertain You Enterprises was doing the food service for one of the venues and most likely somebody noticed our company name on the football foldout and passed it along.

I responded to the attorneys that yes, I had cloned the name from Rich Melman's business and had enjoyed eight years in Chicago dining in his restaurants. But "a lettuce is not a lotus and nobody would confuse a restaurant with a greeting card company." I got back a response that said "okay" but they also warned or asked me to stay away from soliciting restaurants. I laughed when I saw their response because all they had to do was say "boo!" and I would have changed my company name by the end of that day!

For six years when I would say "Lotus Entertain You" the response would be "okay cute name, but what do you do?" It was time for a name change especially since I was now a dot.com. Describing what you do in the name is the right marketing or branding thing to do, not that every company does this. Going only by their name, what does Yahoo or Google do? But there's no mistaking what Toys R Us does or what Ruth's Chris Steakhouse serves for dinner.

I've always enjoyed cute names for businesses and have made the same wrong assumption as a lot of people: cute name = successful business. In 1986 I bought a real cute half-circle table that folded down against the wall. It was perfect for our small kitchen with two barstools for seating. I bought a dozen of them wholesale, created a cute business name of "Your Table Is Ready", ran some ads in local papers, and got no orders. But the name was cute!

I think I got my start in the "cute name" business from my Mom. When she and I were bringing home our first dog from the pound we were thinking of names. She asked, "How about JESSHK? (pronounced Jessick), J for Jeff (me), E for Ellen (Sister), S for Steve (Brother), S for Sy (Dad), H for Harriet (Mom) and K for Karen (Sister)". I loved it! Our dog's name for the vet and licensing was Jesshk, but we called her Jess or Jessie anyway.

So I began thinking of a new name for my business. I've always liked the "only" businesses or the "just" businesses, like "Only Light Bulbs" or "Just Left Socks". Names like these are both descriptive of what the business does, and convey a sense of specialist knowledge of a niche market. A potential consumer expects "Only Light Bulbs" to not only stock whatever light bulb the customer needs, but also to have encyclopedic knowledge of light bulbs.

I wrote five or six variations on paper and as soon as I penned JustPaperRoses the "J P R" jumped off the page at me, like the three letters were magically highlighted. The J was me, Jeff. The P was Phyllis, my Wife (at the time), and the R was Rachel, our Daughter.

So JustPaperRoses.com it was to be! I bought the domain name, filed for a corporate name change, and a few years later registered JustPaperRoses® as a trademark.

PERFECT…well, almost. Many times when I verbally tell someone, "Just Paper Roses dot com" they'll reply, "OK, Paper Roses dot com". I reply, "No the 'just' is in there, Just Paper Roses dot com" and then I spell it for them, "J-U-S-T-P-A-P-E-R-R-O-S-E-S dot com". What many people hear is that it is "just" PaperRoses.com.

In early 2002 my Wife and I divorced, again. Deja-vu? The issues of our first marriage were the same issues of our second marriage, so it was time, again. I already had the business located in a very small (10' x 12') rented office, so I moved to an apartment nearby. For a short time I was again a bachelor flirting with my cocktail napkin roses!

In late 2002 I began dating Deb who I knew first as a customer of JustPaperRoses.com. She was a Director of a department in a hospital, and had ordered personalized JustPaperRoses for each of her over 100 nurses for Nurse's Day plus a second order for holiday gifts.

We married in July, 2003 and had already moved my business to her home in Coconut Creek, Florida.

From our first date my Wife Deb has been a steady source of **_I believe in you_** for both my business and my life. I'm in love with my Wife. I've created a business for spouses who are in love with their spouses, so I believe the energy from my personal relationship carries strongly to my business efforts. Who believes in YOU?

By early 2003 it was evident we had a great business. We were getting a steady order flow for JustPaperRoses with incredible, over-the-top testimonials from our customers. But my "four mentors" had me restless as I knew we were committing a marketing "sin". I knew our customers' dates of their 2nd "cotton" Anniversaries and their email addresses. But, I was doing NOTHING for them.

THE best way to get more business is ALWAYS through past customers as they have already said "yes" to you. Repeat business and referrals from customers are SO important to any business because the cost of gaining a customer the first time is so high.

We ordered real cotton plant stems from a farm in Tennessee thinking that was what we would sell. Well, they were dirty and nasty, nothing we could package and ship to our customers. So we fashioned fake versions, put them on the website on April 1, 2003. I figured I'd be happy if we sold 5 orders for the month. Well, we sold 25 orders that month! The rest of 2003 was spent figuring out how to create "roses" for the first 10 years of Wedding Anniversaries. In 2005 we completed years 11 through 15 with the traditional materials from the Anniversary list.

We now have great repeat business, with many customers coming back to us each year for this year's "rose".

Somebody else created this "tradition" of different materials for the Wedding Anniversary. The list goes in one year increments for years 1 through 15, and then by fives thereafter. In 1922 Emily Post (Miss Manners) wrote an etiquette book in which she named the traditional materials for seven years, 1st-paper, 5th-wood, 10th-(tin) aluminum, 15th-crystal, 20th-china, 25th-silver, 50th-gold. Nobody really knows who filled in the rest.

Here are the years we have covered:

1-paper	6- candy	11- steel	25- silver
2- cotton	7- wool	12- silk	50- gold
3- leather	8- bronze	13- lace	
4- fruit	9- pottery	14- ivory	
5- wood	10- aluminum	15- crystal	

We recently created our own materials for themes for years 16, 17, 18, and 19. Move over Emily Post!

16- wax
17- shell
18- feather
19- bamboo (pending)

I believe in a few years our choices will be listed in every list of "traditional" Wedding Anniversaries. People will ask, "Who in the world created 'feathers' for the 18th Anniversary?" And the answer? "JustPaperRoses.com!"

Almost all our products have morphed over time, some now on their 4th or 5th version. The goal of our product redesign is always to upgrade the presentation while simplifying the design too. We make our products, so minimizing the production time is very important.

1-paper JustPaperRoses®: Our flagship product. I'm almost embarrassed to look at pictures of our original creations, but they sold and brought great testimonials too. For today's version we start with a bright white thin paper and we print our colors with words, clipart or photos on them too. We twirl the paper, twist the base, wrap a floral wire around it, and then twirl the wire with floral tape, feeding in a silk leaf midway down the stem.

1-paper Lifelike Paper Roses™: these are imported paper rose heads we attach to our floral stems.

1-paper Origami Orchids (in my pocket, photo back cover): NO you won't see these on our website. I stopped selling them four years ago because they require my own finger time to create. I created three size arrangements, with the largest selling for $200, and they sold well. Over 10 years ago I received an order to send one to Japan. I laughed at the time because sending Origami to Japan is like sending sand to the Sahara. A few years ago I found an American artist creating my identical version, even using the same paper. I don't have any claim on the Origami Orchid blossom itself as it's a very old Origami model. But the way I fashioned it on wires with a central purple tassel and then "planted" on a base, was my original styling.

I contacted the artist and was told this was taught to him by an old Japanese man and "these are all over Japan!" Too funny. I have no issue with the "clones" and I'm happy I could indirectly teach so many people to create such beautiful flowers.

Imitation really is the sincerest form of flattery!

2-cotton JustCottonRoses™: We glue standard cotton balls in the center of our fine silk roses.

3-leather JustLeatherRoses™: Strips of leather twirled to fashion a leather rose, created by our friends at MapleLeather.com. We put the leaves on each stem.

4-fruit JustFruitRoses™: We glue artificial fruits in the center of our fine silk roses.

5-wood JustWoodRoses™: Our wood rose heads are carved by hand just for us in Indonesia. We put our rose heads (red, yellow, or purple) on our floral stems. Next year we'll add a natural wood option too.

5-wood Bloodwood Rose: ***magnificent!*** Created by our friends at OilsWoodStone.com.

6-candy JustCandyRoses™: Candy button strips twirled the same way we make JustPaperRoses.

7-wool JustWoolRoses™: Strips of pure lamb's wool rolled and then attached to our floral stems. The lamb's wool is from a drugstore, used as a foot-care product! CVS employees chuckle each time we order 50 bags.

8-bronze JustBronzeRoses™: Bronze wool cut, rolled into a ball and glued into the center of our fine silk roses.

9-pottery JustPotteryRoses™: Created by our friends at StoneRoses.biz. We add a leaf to the stem.

10-aluminum JustAluminumRoses™: We die cut squares of aluminum and form the blossoms by hand, which are then attached to our floral stems.

11-steel JustSteelRoses™: Steel wool cut, rolled into a ball and glued into the center of our fine silk roses.

11-Lifelike JustSteelRoses™: *awesome!* Created by our friends at TracyMaisel.com.

12-silk JustSilkRoses™: Our fine silk roses.

13-lace JustLaceRoses™: Strips of lace cut and twirled similar to JustPaperRoses, attached to our floral stems.

14-ivory JustTaguaNutRoses™: *amazing!*

My #1 pick for our most unique rose!
Tagua nut rose heads carved for us (modeled from our JustWoodRoses) in Ecuador, attached to our floral stems. Tagua nuts are called "fake" ivory.

No need to kill an elephant just to make JustIvoryRoses!

15-crystal JustCrystalRoses™: Hand blown glass roses from Lithuania.

16-wax (new) JustCandleRoses™: Rose candle on a floral wire stem, tape wrapped with our leaf added.

17-shell (new) JustShellRoses™: Painted red shell on floral stem with painted green shells for leaves.

18-feather (new) JustFeatherRoses™: Roses fashioned from dyed red goose feathers with leaves of dyed green goose feathers.

19-bamboo (pending) JustBambooRoses™: Roses made from bamboo just for us in Indonesia.

25-silver JustSilverPaperRoses™: Our personalized JustPaperRoses made from silver matte paper.

50-gold JustGoldPaperRoses™: Our personalized JustPaperRoses made from gold matte paper.

EACH floral product is beautifully packaged in a standard clear long-stem rose box, with green tissue paper, ribbons and iridescent shred for a GREAT gift presentation!

Our silk roses and our floral stems (cover photo) are of the highest quality. When I look at our silk roses without my reading glasses I'd think they were real. The stems even have a "scar nub" which looks like what a real rose stem looks like when a thorn is broken off. The stem itself isn't just green, it's green with brownish-red tones running throughout looking again just like a real rose stem. The leaves look like real leaves.

For the few who look at our products and say or think "I can make these" or "I can make these cheaper" I would first sarcastically respond, "Well, I could make my own car too, but I think GM makes a better Corvette than I could!" But more modestly, I'd advise them to go price the best looking silk stems in their local crafts or floral store – they're not cheap!

Our floral stems are a funny story. When making any artificial flower we have to figure out how to create a stem and/or attach a blossom to a stem. The choices are limited – standard floral wire, wood spike stem, or a floral stem. The only way to get a floral stem is to buy a silk rose and throw away the blossom! We would "strip" stems to salvage the stem with leaves attached, sepal (green part just below the blossom), and a core pin which is essential to anchor any of our creations to the stem. The sepal was glued to the silk blossom so "stripping" was a lot like peeling potatoes and the prep work was laborious.

It just seemed funny to me that we were taking apart silk roses when the pieces we needed were sitting in a factory somewhere in China awaiting assembly. I contacted my floral supply company and their first response was, "it's really not that simple" with a reluctance to want to get it done. About a year later I contacted them again this time offering, "I'll pay you the same price as the stem I'm stripping and I'll put in an order for $5K to $10K. Reorders will be the same size."

We got it done. We don't strip stems anymore!

Chapter 11
Johnny Badass Romantic!

"Good entrepreneurs are not, per se, lucky or smart.
They are just smart enough
to realize when they are getting lucky."
Bo Peabody
Lucky or Smart?

Bo Peabody goes on to add, "It's a subtle but very important distinction." I've quoted my own version many times, "Gold falls onto all our laps from time to time, but most of us are too busy to even notice!" Other people subscribe to the philosophy of "you make your own luck." Would *you* rather be lucky? Or smart?

"The sure way to miss success
is to miss the opportunity."
Victor Charles

Sometime in the year 2000 I received my very first emailed testimonial which included the words:

"…she cried…"

I wish I could tell you I printed that testimonial and have it framed on my wall, but I don't. That email was also the *exact moment* when:

I knew what I wanted to be when I grew up!

YEAH!!! 45 years old and I finally knew!!!

Sometimes one is smart enough to know when they've gotten lucky on the spot, at the moment it happens. Other times it's only known after the fact, sometimes a long time after the fact. While I enjoyed twirling cocktail napkin roses for "social purposes" for many years, who-da-thunk that my friend Jay showing me how to twirl a cocktail napkin rose would morph into a business ten years later? At the moment he was teaching me to twirl my first cocktail napkin rose I had NO idea just how lucky I was.

But "…she cried…" was instantaneous. I was smart enough to know I had just gotten lucky and immediately identified this as my "inch of daylight". For a few moments I was taken aback. "…she cried…" is a very, very powerful testimonial. Our paper roses might be nice, but they are *not* destined for art museums.

So I thought about it some more and now describe what I call a "romantic setup". The couple had dated for a while, and now has been happily married for one year. The Wife **knows** her Husband is "lovingly clueless" when it comes to getting her birthday and holiday gifts. Somebody created the tradition of "paper" for the 1st Wedding Anniversary. The Wife most likely knows the 1st is "paper" and she probably highly doubts her Husband knows this.

And then,… here he comes with a clear long-stem rose box in his arms. He hands it to her and she sees immediately that these are paper roses (usually in red) printed with their names, 1st Anniversary, and date. She reads the gift tag "Happy 1st "paper" Anniversary", and

"…she cries…"

Oh, the thoughtfulness of her "lovingly clueless" Husband! He didn't just grab a dozen fresh roses at a convenience store on his way home from work. He searched for and found the perfect "paper" gift for the occasion, and it is personalized, and it is flowers, and they will last forever!

I was smart enough to know that I had just gotten lucky. Now, business success would be a "mere" marketing task. This very first "…she cried…" testimonial was from a Husband who most likely was just like all the other Husbands out there, and his Wife was most likely just like all the other Wives out there. So my task became, "if one Wife cried, then thousands more will…" if I can only find them or more accurately, if they can only find me!

Now you know why I'm "just a crab with good marketing". Like Hawthorne the crab in the cartoon "…the participant's state of emotion has been briefly altered…in one fleeting moment art has been created…". Again, it's not that the product has become "art". The "art" is the Husband getting the sought after reaction from his Wife! Since that first "…she cried…" testimonial we've received hundreds more that include those words and thousands more that include words such as "awesome…I was her hero…you made my day…her reaction was priceless…a BIG hit…", etc.

One Husband thanked us for helping him be
"Johnny Romantic Badass!"

In a testimonial for our 5th Anniversary JustWoodRoses a Husband wrote, "I came home from work and she had the JustWoodRoses in her arms. She put the baby to sleep and then it was all a blur like a second honeymoon. You guys should sell energizer pills with these!"

I couldn't stop laughing. From that moment I've been telling people that the G-rated version of what I do is, "I help a Husband create a romantic Anniversary night." The R-rated version is what I tell my Wife, "YOU are responsible only for ONE man having great sex on his Wedding Anniversary night. I think I'm responsible…

…for THOUSANDS!"

My most incredible story of being smart enough to know when I got lucky was with my now "last" Wife, Deb. She was foolish enough to say "yes". I knew I had gotten lucky, because I was smart enough to ask her the question before she *really* got to know me!

Toilet Paper! Yes, Toilet Paper!
In 2008 we sold 1,400 rolls of toilet paper. No shit!

In the spring of 2007 I received a phone call from a VP at 800-FLOWERS.COM® asking the proverbial "would you ever consider being bought out?" To which the answer is the proverbial "does a bear…?" We never got together after an initial conversation or two, but I put in writing some of my ideas for future new products.

One idea was "Happy 1st 'Paper' Anniversary" printed on a roll of toilet paper. I knew there are specialty printers that can print anything you wish on TP. It was a backburner idea for me for at least four years. At the time, about 80% of our customers were Husbands, so I figured the TP would be a cute gag gift add-on to an order, priced at $14.95 per roll with no increase in shipping cost.

Committing an idea to paper can be so powerful! Now I had to find out if TP would sell. So in June 2007 I ordered ten rolls and put the new item for sale on our website. *TEN MINUTES* after it was online we got our first order…and it was a female buyer…and the TP was the only thing she ordered so she paid shipping charges too!

By the end of the week we sold out of our ten rolls and eight of them were to women ordering only the TP!

I had been viewing my business erroneously. I assumed since 80% of my customers were men, then 80% of the visitors to our site were men. This turns out to be false. Many Wives wouldn't buy our flowers for their Husbands so many female visitors to our site left without a purchase. Visitors to our site are most likely 50/50 men/women and now we had something "special" for Wives! Toilet paper!!!

I took the TP offline to order 80 more rolls and put them back online for August 2007 when we sold 90 rolls. I reordered after the 1st week sales were 25 rolls! Since then we've added 10 more varieties of sayings, but the best seller is the 1st Anniversary TP. We sell about 100 rolls per month and 80% of these sales are to women. A few have paid up to $80 so they could get it delivered by UPS the next day. Now we get great "he laughed…" testimonials, and some "best laugh I ever got out of him" too. One wrote, "He couldn't stop laughing all day, each time he walked by the bathroom!" I'm just waiting for a testimonial that says "he laughed when he saw the toilet paper but took a crap when he saw the credit card bill!"

Now we have a 50/50 customer mix. Tapping into the female market for us means things like more referrals – women tend to refer to their friends better than men do. Also a woman is more likely to come back to order our Sweet 16 JustPaperRoses or Birthday JustPaperRoses.

NOBODY is more surprised than us about the amount of toilet paper we sell. My Wife simply observed, "Women have a sense of humor too!" I replied, "Yeah I know, but this is a gag gift,…bathroom humor. I had no idea that it would be something so many women would do!"

The crab with good marketing learned something new!

"…he laughed…"

is my 2nd , inch of daylight. I'm just smart enough to realize I got lucky again, for a 2nd time. Now we also sell on the power of humor, another strong emotion.

There have been many times when I've thought I was at the "end of my road" for creativity for new products.

Then,… I get lucky again!

Is this book my 3rd, inch of daylight?

Part 3
Deer in my backyard,
Corvette in my garage

*"Don't tell me money doesn't buy happiness.
I'd rather find out myself!"*
Seen on a t-shirt

If it was "a pickup truck in my driveway" then we'd have a name for a country song! This book is NOT a story about getting rich, but I now understand the adage, "wealthy people are just broke at a higher level!" Money comes in faster but it goes out faster too. As fast as a Corvette!

Chapter 12
Money, Money, Money

*"With money in your pocket you are wise
and you are handsome and you sing well too!"*
Yiddush proverb

Money, or more precisely gaining money, really is a
mind-set. It is **not** that difficult to make money. But it is
VERY difficult to keep it! Nobody truly "has" money.
We all have control of a certain amount of money.
Some have control of little or no money and others have
control of large or very large amounts. Here is a
Universal Principle: when you demonstrate skill with
whatever amount is currently available to you, more will
arrive. Of course, NEVER as soon as you think it should!

*"Money is a terrible master
But an excellent servant"*
P.T. Barnum

My very first experience of money awareness was at age 5 when for some reason I was dropped off to be babysat at my Grandfather's jewelry factory. Norma, an office secretary, gave me a task of alphabetizing her files. When it came time for me to leave, my Grandfather gave me a $20 bill for the "work" I had done! Adjusted for inflation this would be about $140 today! I was hooked! Why does a kid need kindergarten when he can make $20 just for sitting on Norma's lap and alphabetizing some files?

Today my Granddaughters do some work for me too, unpacking boxes, sticker labeling our vases, and even making some products. I pay them $2. I can't imagine handing out $100 bills, and I have a *big* imagination!

From my age 3 to 8 there was a TV show called, "Bachelor Father" and from age 1 to 6 there was another TV show called "The Millionaire". I liked both the ideas of being a bachelor with kids, and also of being a millionaire.
I announced to my family, "When I grow up I'm going to be a 'millionaire spatula!'" My family teased me for years.

When I was 10 I took over another boy's paper route just for a summer while he was away with his family. It was a before sunrise, morning route, six days per week with the Sunday delivery going to the evening paper route boy.
The Providence Journal had both a morning and evening edition! The weekly cost was 35 cents and collection day was Saturday with some customers leaving money in an envelope and others requiring a knock on their door.

Many customers gave me 2 quarters, a 15 cent or 43% tip.
My first week collecting I had so much change in my
shorts pockets that when I stood on the pedals of my
bicycle to pedal, my shorts kept dropping!

Now THAT's money awareness!

Near the end of the summer the newspaper raised their
weekly rate to 50 cents and my tips dropped to nothing,
a nickel, or a dime. No more 43% tippers. People who
receive tips are not usually the business owner, so it's
difficult to rig the prices for optimal tips, but I would think
I'd rather be a bartender with beer costing $2.25 than $2.75
– most customers will pay the same $3.00 either way.

From ages 10 through 15, I would do a little grass mowing
in summer and snow shoveling in the winter, and while I
liked the money, I really didn't like the work. I learned the
risk of quoting by the job when after a particularly heavy
and wet snowfall a regular customer's driveway and
sidewalk took me six hours to clear when it would usually
be two hours. Another neighbor whose lawn I mowed was
very particular and fussy making me re-do the edging when
it wasn't to his liking, and it was never to his liking.

Before age 10 I had opened my own savings account in our
local bank and I made deposits of as little as 50 cents.
I was fascinated by the concept of getting interest on my
money, something for nothing! At the end of each quarter,
even if I didn't have a deposit, I would go to the bank with
my passbook so they could post my interest earned!

My brother had started a coin collection which I took over with my own additions. I would go to the bank and exchange cash for rolls of pennies, nickels, dimes and quarters and in those days you could find numismatic value coins just in your change. I was turned on by the money awareness of certain coins being worth more than their face value, and since I was just finding these coins myself, there was no cost other than my time. I never purchased a coin to add to the collection. Even after the phase-out of silver coins in 1964 it took about five or six years before it became a rarity to not find at least one silver coin in a roll of change. When silver prices soared in the late 70's I sold the silver coins for $1,000.

At age 15 ½, I got my first "real" job at Burger King. In 1969 the first Burger King in New England was opened in Cranston R.I. by Nick Janikies. McDonald's had no locations but there was a Burger Chef and a few other fledgling hamburger stands. My older Sister started working at BK in 1969 so by the summer of 1970 I had an "in" and I was hired even though I wasn't yet 16. For my first few weeks Nick had me working on the landscaping with another of his employees. Then he brought me inside. I liked the work. We were always busy serving customers, prepping food in the back, or cleaning the dining area or parking lot. Nick even sent us down the adjacent residential streets to pick up any litter left behind by his customers. Nick was in the store every day, probably 12 hours per day or more. I learned quite a few things from him and picked up a few more things by observation too.

In the year I worked for Nick he opened his 2nd and 3rd locations. When I started, employees on their own lunch or dinner breaks could prepare and eat whatever they wanted. We were teenagers and for me it was not uncommon to make a triple Whopper with a three sides of fries and a shake with two refills. Soon employee food became regimented and we had to get our food up front like a customer and we could only order a limited quantity. By this time it was OK with me because I had gotten sick of hamburgers and had started to take my meals from home. Tuna fish and peanut butter & jelly started to taste great! Maybe in food service it's a good idea to give employees all they can eat and just let them get tired of your food? But the lesson was that teenage employees can literally eat your profits, so "all-you-can-eat" on breaks had to go!

I noticed McDonalds opening just down the street from each of Nick's three stores and commented to him, "Does McDonalds have a real estate location department? Or do they just find a spot down the street from you?" to which he responded, "It's great, more business for both of us!" I learned that the bigger task for the hamburger fast food chains was to create awareness for their market, so their customers would go out to eat out more and more.

At JustPaperRoses.com our overall marketing task is to create awareness of the material themes for Wedding Anniversaries…did you know the 1st is 'paper', 2nd is 'cotton', etc.? If a consumer becomes aware of the themes and buys a different product in the traditional material from someone else, that's OK with us.

Our website links to some of our vendors and we invite our customer to visit their sites to see what else they create with traditional Anniversary materials. When the market niche grows, we all share more and more happy customers!

One "sleight of hand" marketing magic I saw at Burger King was in drink pricing. Originally the drink size choices were "regular & large". One day the menu board was changed to "regular & small". They were the same sized drinks and prices, but now if you didn't ask for a "small" you got the larger more expensive drink.

I saw a similar sleight of hand with the Florida Lotto years ago. When they started, the billboards said "$4 million" which was $200K for 20 years. Then one day they changed it to "$6 million" by making the $200K annual payments for 30 years. The annuity cost only slightly more for the State of Florida since the present value of payments in years 20 through 30 are close to zero, but now they could billboard a higher value! Magic! I'm surprised a State hasn't created a "$1 BILLION" lotto jackpot, $1,000,000 per year…for 1,000 years!

While not sleight of hand, I recently added a more expensive version of our wood vases for the customer who wants to spend a little more. To my surprise 40% of sales of our wood vases are now the more expensive version. Give a customer a chance to spend more…and they just might! Marketing is all about guiding a prospective customer to their own highest possible perceived value.

I moved quickly up in position at Burger King, to the top position of working the "front board" where all the "have it your ways" are created on demand and quickly. I could hear the order called out and have it ready by the time the cashier finished taking the customer's money. But my ultimate favorite position was when I got to work the customer window, handling the money. In 1970 smart cash registers hadn't yet been invented. We took the orders on preprinted pads of paper. I could tally the total in my head and know the change needed as soon as the customer handed me their bills. Best of all, we had one of those change machines which loaded stacks of coins vertically and as soon as the manager loaded a new roll I could see the silver dimes and quarters. I'd race to swap them out for my own change before anyone else saw them!

In 1970 Nick was in his early 30s, an ex-accountant with a beat up station wagon. By the time I left him one year later he had a new Lincoln Mark III and was building his dream home for his family. Before I left to start my senior year in high school (and my next afterschool job) Nick took me aside and suggested or offered that I should stay on with him as a manager and not go to college. I turned him down knowing my parents would kill me if I told them I wasn't interested in going to college. Nick became a huge success story within Burger King, today owning over 80 BKs as well as other restaurants and country clubs too! I'm glad I'm not in the restaurant business, but do sometimes wonder where I'd be had I taken Nick up on his offer?

My last high school job was with James Kaplan's Jewelers, a local jewelry and gift store. James Kaplan was a traditional fine jewelry and diamond expert, and his Son Jerry was the entrepreneur who expanded the store to include cameras, TVs, stereos, luggage, china, silverware, glassware, giftware, etc. I started with Jerry just as they were moving to a newly built store six times larger than the old location. I started in the stockroom. I liked it. This was before computers. Salespeople would have to call downstairs to inquire if certain items or certain pieces, patterns, or colors were in stock. Soon I would know, without having to check the shelves, what was in stock and what was not. By holiday time Jerry asked me to wear a jacket and tie and come upstairs to be a salesperson. I liked this too. Jerry was a people magnet, handling customers much the same way as my Grandpa. He was a bundle of energy, never stopping. One day I saw him walking across the store with two employees and four customers trailing behind him like baby ducklings.

I knew the prices Jerry paid for almost everything because invoices were included with everything that came into the stockroom. I saw that he paid $400 for a Sony TV and was selling it for $420. I saw he ran a promotional for GE toaster ovens on sale at $18.95 when I knew he paid $20 for them. I once asked him about this as we stood near the center of the store, near the quarter of the store that was the fine jewelry department. Jerry said to me, "See all this?" as he pointed to the other three-quarters of the store, "This is *all* so a customer might stop and buy a piece of jewelry on their way out!"

In my business today I think about that lesson from Jerry each time a customer order is for a 1-stem or just for one roll of toilet paper. Our internet store has lots of traffic and of course we would like all orders to be big. But our customers who order small orders might be back for more, and they might bring friends and family with them too!

The Kaplan's business thrived in the new location. Their reputation in the local area was tops, over the tops. Jerry not only had the only Porsche in town, but it was mustard yellow so you knew when he was coming. He worked hard and played hard with his family. When I was in college I got news in a phone call from my Mom that Jerry and his Wife had died in a crash of a private plane. Jerry was the pilot and his Wife was the only passenger. Their family was devastated and not too long afterwards the business was closed. Any family businesses can be "best of times, worst of times" for lots of reasons, and this was indeed a tragic ending to a family business story.

So my money awareness as a kid and teenager had me always with a few bucks in my pocket. My after school activity was a job instead of sports or a school club. When I was dating I enjoyed not having to worry about paying for the dinner, movie or gas for the car. My standard of living was probably at my lifetime highest during high school!

Money awareness is central to being an entrepreneur. I once listened to a speaker who asked his audience, "By a show of hands, how many here want to make a million dollars? (hands go up) Now by keeping your hand up, how many of you are really saying that you want to *SPEND* a million dollars?" He went on to say that you won't ever make a million dollars if your only motivation is that you want to buy nice stuff. The challenge of growing a business is what drives an entrepreneur and yes, money really is just a way to keep score.

Speaking of driving…

Yes, there is a 2009 Corvette in our garage and my Wife drives it to her work every day. I'm not telling you this to boast in any way, nor discuss buying material stuff as a measure for your success. But none of us is getting any younger. I'm 55 and you've read about my early life troubles. At 45 I knew what I wanted to be when I grew up and now ten years later I'm starting to treat myself in the manner to which I'd like to become accustomed! My Wife and I can afford two middle priced cars or one real nice car and one beater. My 2000 Mitsubishi Eclipse with 110,000 miles is the beater. I use my car for runs to my storage bay to get shipping boxes, for runs taking cardboard and recyclables to the local trash dump, and for local business errands. When together with my Wife we enjoy driving the nice car. Traded in for the Corvette was our 2003 Jaguar S-type which we bought in 2005. It had 18,000 miles and was in Jaguar's pre-owned program. GREAT car too!

Even the Corvette has yet another "I can't quite explain it" story. In late 2008 I began "manifesting" a Corvette by putting a picture of a black on black coupe on my desk. I was thinking 2010 or 2011 for a new Corvette. Then GM and the economy started their nosedives. I was worried that GM might stop making Corvettes so I started looking online for a used 2008 or 2009 with under 20,000 miles. I talked to a dealer who has 36 years experience buying and selling used Corvettes exclusively. He told me I wasn't alone in the market for a used Corvette as his sales were brisk with many people thinking this might be their last chance to buy a Corvette too. Then in March 2009, I accompanied my Wife on one of her business seminar meetings in Atlanta. On a Thursday it was miserably raining and while I planned to browse in the mall across the street, I now really didn't feel like mall shopping.

So I decided to find a Chevy dealer and go waste his time.

I walked in to the showroom and the receptionist called over their Corvette specialist. He walked up to me while I was looking out the front window, through the pouring rain, at the row of cars parked right up front. There was not one, but two black on black coupes. I asked, "What's with those two?" He said, pointing to the one on the left, "That one is Jeff's car. It's a 2009 with 5,500 miles on it." I asked, "What do you mean 'Jeff's car'!?!? I'M Jeff!" (we hadn't yet introduced ourselves). He then told me of Jeff S___, who buys a new GM car every six months. He's not a real rich guy, but has a GM employee discount card and he hates putting on miles on the cars he buys!

We drove the Jag to Atlanta and drove home in…

"Jeff's" Corvette!

A lesson to all who take their spouse on business trips – beware of leaving a spouse with nothing to do!

My picture of the Corvette on my desk manifested to the real car in my garage! Can you really get whatever you want in life by just helping enough people get what they want? If my Psychologist on March 17, 1993 had said "Jeff, if you just help 30,000 people by creating great Anniversary gifts you'll be able to buy a Corvette sixteen years from now", would I have believed her?

No, and I would have found a new psychologist too!

I would have created gifts for 30,000 customers even if it didn't result in a Corvette. I would have created their gifts

BECAUSE…

Now I knew what I wanted to be when I grew up!!!

Chapter 13
So, You Wanna be an Entrepreneur?

"What do you invest in?" I asked.
"Whatever pays a profit," he answered.
"That's no strategy," I retorted as I left his yacht.
Anonymous

So, you wanna be an entrepreneur? Are you crazy? Nuts? Maybe this should be a one page chapter because being an entrepreneur is like what it says on a Harley-Davidson t-shirt, "If I have to explain it, you wouldn't understand!"

"Always tell yourself:
The difference between running a business
and ruining a business is i "
Frank Tyger

Just what is an "entrepreneur"?

In 1987 I joined a group named "Young Entrepreneurs". One of our monthly meetings was hosted in a local hotel and the hotel owner was the guest speaker. The meeting room was set up for a typical conference meeting, single rows of narrow tables and chairs with a drinking glass upside down on the table at each seat, and a communal pitcher of ice water on each table. The speaker introduced himself and started his chat about entrepreneurship. As he was standing in front of the first row of tables he said,

> "An entrepreneur is someone who has
> …personal…financial…risk."

He had absentmindedly put his hand on the upside down base of a drinking glass right in front of him, and with each word "personal… financial… risk", he lifted the glass slightly and rapped it on the table for emphasis and on the word "risk" the glass broke. He looked down, now aware of what he had done and without hesitation said, "That just cost me $2". By the look on his face I knew he hadn't broken the glass on purpose. An entrepreneur is NOT somebody who purposely wastes their own money. When money is wasted an entrepreneur takes it personally, very personally! A direct hit to YOUR wallet.

Wait.

Do you hear that flushing noise?

Listen closely. Yep, that's YOUR money being flushed down the toilet. Is it ALL of your money? Well in some cases, yes. It's not unusual at all to hear stories of people who committed and lost their entire life savings in a restaurant or other small business. I did it with my floor trading. But even if you don't lose it all, not a year will go by that you won't have the experience of at least some of your money being flushed away.

They say (just who is "they" anyway?) that before you buy a boat you should go to a dock, take out a $100 bill, crumple it up and throw it in the water. If you don't jump in after it then you have what it takes to own a boat. Did I do this before I bought my first (and last) boat? No, but if I did, it would have saved me thousands of dollars at the small cost of only getting wet once!

How will you deal with your losses of money? Can you right now take a $100 bill, crumple it up and go flush it down your toilet? Did I do this? Well, not exactly but I do have a $100 bill that I folded (from instructions) into an incredible 6-pointed Star of David. It's on my desk, framed behind glass, with writing on the background that says,

"In Emergency BREAK GLASS"

I look at this $100 bill daily as a $100 bill that I can't touch, one that I've taken out of circulation. While not quite down the toilet, it is a daily visual reminder of money that used to belong to me!

No, being an entrepreneur isn't all about losing money.
Maybe the best metaphor is the game of poker with your
stack of chips in front of you. Your stack grows and
shrinks and your long term goal is to grow your stack.
But some days you just don't get dealt good cards and
some days you just get beat no matter what good cards
are dealt to you. Yeah, like Kenny Rogers sings (written
by Don Schlitz) in The Gambler:

> *"You got to know when to hold em, know when to fold em.*
> *Know when to walk away and know when to run.*
> *You never count your money when you're sittin at the table.*
> *There'll be time enough for countin when the dealins done."*

This is YOUR money we are talking about. When you set
up your office, do you need a new desk? Or would a used
desk suffice? Or does a plank of wood across several
cinder blocks work for you? We reuse packing material
that comes from our incoming supplies to save a few bucks
plus get at least one more use of plastic material before it
might go to a garbage dump. I'm not necessarily
suggesting you be miserly about every spending decision,
but be aware that it is YOUR money you are spending.
The *business* is not spending and risking money, YOU are!

It would be very unfair for me to dismiss any and all
employees, but an employee is at least one step removed
from the money spent by a business, money that many
times is within the employee's authorization to spend.
My question when I worked at Xerox of "why are we on
overtime?" to get a response of "because it's in the budget"
is just something that would not happen if the money

belonged to the person who approved the budget. An entrepreneur will NEVER pay for overtime unless the workload absolutely demands overtime. Paying more for labor is only an option of last resort.

In our business we take advantage of economies of scale, buying in bulk or case quantities wherever we can. I look forward to the day when my order from my Indonesian source can be at least a half-container or even full-container load to minimize the shipping cost per item. I joke with my UPS drivers that I look forward to the day when they have to back an 18-wheeler up my driveway! Before the 18-wheeler I'd like to at least see the day where they drop off a small empty trailer and pick up our full trailer each day. UPS does discount for volume.

Take advantage of credit cards. It took me until 2005 to clean up my credit scores but now that I have high scores I have a business line of credit with an interest rate of 1% over the prime rate. I also have a business American Express card that has no fees and pays back 2% cash of every purchase. I charge as many of my vendor purchases as possible on this card. This year we will <u>get back</u> about $3,000 on purchases we would have made anyway! I take advantage of credit cards that offer zero interest for 6 or 12 months. It's FREE money on which I pay the required monthly minimum and then pay off completely as soon as the introductory time period lapses. Do NOT pay interest as that is just more money being flushed away.

If your business is carrying monthly credit card balances requiring interest payments it is a red flag, a symptom that your business is NOT as profitable as you think it is. The only exception is during a startup phase where paying interest on credit card balances might be the only way to launch the business. If this is the case, then paying down your debt gets the highest of priorities.

Borrowed money is VERY expensive.

Take advantage of technology. In January 2005 I made the most difficult phone call of my business career.

"You're fired!" I told my web person.

She had been my web person for four years and had done a GREAT job. So why did I have to fire her? Our website had reached the point where I needed to be able to manage it myself, changing products, photos, prices, and website wording instantly, and as frequently as necessary. More importantly we had three areas of the business that weren't "talking" to each other. An order starts in the website shopping cart which then emails an order confirmation to us and to you. Customer information needs to be stored in what is called a CRM, customer resource manager. On the day of fulfillment a UPS shipping label must be generated. We would get an order from the website, type the customer data into ACT! (CRM), and on the day of fulfillment again type the same information into UPS Worldship. There were more than a few days when just typing shipping labels took two to three hours of my, or my assistant's, time.

We signed on with NetSuite.com which is like sharing a huge IT (information technology) department. NetSuite does what big companies do in-house. All of NetSuite's customers share the platform. NetSuite is an ASP (application service provider) where we pay monthly, and our website and business resides on their servers and on their IT platform. An additional advantage is we can log on to our NetSuite account from any computer in the world and see what is going on with our business. Now, when a customer orders at the website, their information is automatically entered in the NetSuite CRM. But my most *glorious* moment is when each morning we fulfill orders. NetSuite is integrated with UPS. We simply go to a bulk fulfillment NetSuite screen, click a checkbox of each order we want to fulfill, click "print labels" and our UPS thermal label printer spits off label after label after label. We ship 25 orders per day, but on our busiest day this year, before Valentine's Day, I watched in pure joy as 91 labels printed in rapid fire. The UPS and CRM integration with NetSuite saves us about a half of an employee's wages per month.

"Tech" can be and usually is mind boggling. My first words to tech people in my life are "I'm 55 and went into engineering school in 1972 with a slide rule and came out in 1976 with a Bowmar calculator that could add, subtract, multiply, divide, and take a square root. I've written programs, but not since 1978, so I'm a good customer for you. I understand the power of a computer, what it can do and how it does it. But please,

DO NOT TALK "TECH" TO ME!

Having a business today automatically means you will need some level of tech, even if you don't have a website. Paying for tech help is very expensive so it's a given that the more you, or a partner or employee of your business, understands tech the better off you will be. The good news is almost all services come with user tutorials and online user forums. It's still mind boggling to me!

The home office.

Jeff Zbar of ChiefHomeOfficer.com has made his career writing about the home office. Rather than regurgitating his wisdom and advice here, do check out his website. He's another great example of creating a career within a niche of his own interest. He's been writing about the home office since 1989. Recently Marriott's Residence Inn tapped Jeff to be in an advertisement featuring him and his tips for your office on the road. This ad will be seen by millions of people. Jeff loves what he does, and it shows.

I "pioneered" my own home office in 1984 so when I started Lotus Entertain You, Inc. it was only natural to work from a home office. The business couldn't support renting an office anyway. I've had four home offices since 1994 and there have been many times when I felt the need to "bust out", in a good way. Spending all day every day in the home can get a little claustrophobic. It's not unusual for my Wife to come home from her work and I say, "Take me out to dinner, anywhere! I gotta get out of here!"

Just before our move here to Milledgeville I checked local office rents. Back in Florida at a going away party for us, I said to the Dad of a friend, a man with whom I've had a few small business chats, "In Milledgeville we can rent a 750 sq.ft. office for only $500 per month." The same office in Ft. Lauderdale would be about $2,000 per month. My view was that it's so cheap to rent an office here, why not? His response without hesitation? "Don't you have something better to do with $6,000 per year?" Two years later we're still in our home office! I'm not sure of the whereabouts of the $12,000 we "saved", but I do know that office rent is overhead we just don't need right now.

Our last two homes were nicely set up for a home business. Our home in Ft. Lauderdale is 50 years old and one of the prior owners had added a 350 sq.ft. "bonus" room. Our backyard is on an ocean access canal. My desk looked out the window on our Florida tropical landscaping and a dock with our 26' sailboat. How's that for an office view?

Our move to small town Georgia was sticker-shock in reverse, or like Wal-Mart says, rollback pricing! To give a good comparison, our 10' x 20' storage bay for our shipping boxes and other supplies was $240 per month in Ft. Lauderdale. Here in Milledgeville the same 10' x 20' is $85 per month. Our home is on a wooded acre and above the garage is our 300 sq.ft. "bonus" room. My view out the window above my desk is of trees and deer! Yep deer in my backyard, especially when I put corn out for them to eat. Another great home office set up!

146

If you don't have a bonus room then a spare bedroom,
basement, or your garage might work as well.

One great advantage of a business that is 100% on the
internet is you can take it with you almost wherever you
wish to live. In Ft. Lauderdale on October 31, 2007 after
UPS had picked up for our last time there, I unplugged my
computer and telephone and packed them in my car. On
Thursday the movers came and packed up by 2 p.m. I put
our three cats in cat-carriers, put them in my car, and hit the
road. Ten hours later I was in our new home. The second
thing I did, after setting up the kitty litter, was to plug in
the computer and phone to make sure we were all set to go.
Everything worked fine. Friday the movers arrived and
unloaded. Saturday Deb got here in her car. On Monday
we were shipping from Milledgeville, Georgia y'all!
We only missed two shipping days and our customers had
no idea that we had moved, nor would they even care!

Speaking of cats,

The home office has "all the comforts of home" literally.
In my earlier days of this business I used to compare it to
my limo driving days where it took 12 hours of being on
call to earn 8 hours of pay. Similarly I would tell people it
took me 12 hours to get in 8 hours of work because I would
take the dog for a walk, take a nap, exercise with my
Bowflex®, putter around the house and/or garden doing
chores, run errands, etc. At our level of business today it
now takes me 12 hours to get in 12 hours of work, as our
customers have become my bosses keeping me very busy!

But working from home makes it easier, much easier.
There is no commute so I start at 6:00 a.m. in my bathrobe
(more information than you needed to know?) checking
emails and orders that came in overnight. I still take lots of
mini-breaks to do things around the house, feed the deer,
take a nap, run errands, or just play with our now four cats.

Our move itself while not quite an "I can't explain this",
is a story of committing to something first, and THEN the
pieces of the puzzle fall into place. We decided to move to
Milledgeville, home to our five Granddaughters, in mid
2006, of course right after the housing market had peaked.
My Wife's career is managing nurses in a hospital. In
Florida she was always getting calls from head-hunters.
After a frustrating year with no interested buyers for our
home I said to Deb, "I don't want to put our lives on hold
awaiting the sale of the house. If you can get a similar
position to yours in Georgia let's move, even if we have to
continue paying a mortgage on the empty house."

By August of 2007 Deb had several interviews with a
hospital in Augusta, which is about a two hour drive from
here, so "doable" in terms of being close enough to family
to see them often. I asked her, "What about that one
hospital in Milledgeville, Oconee Regional?" She replied
with an attitude, "Oh, I sent them my resume in January
and I never heard anything from them." I went online
myself to Oconee's website, found their nurse job openings
posted, and my heart skipped three beats when I saw her
same management position listed as vacant since June!

This is ONE position in a ONE hospital town so the chance of this position being vacant at any given point in time is extremely small. Deb sent her resume and in September 2007 we visited here, she interviewed and was given an offer which she accepted on the spot. We submitted a bid on our house which was accepted. At the same time a woman saw our Florida home advertised for sale or rent and she wanted to rent! She is now our tenant.

How many people trudge through life saying things like "when such-and-such happens, THEN I'd do such-and-such?" I always hear lots of people say, "When we have extra money, we'll…" and I always ask, "What's that? What is this 'extra' money you speak about? And how can I get some?" I've heard an adage "life starts when the kids go off to college and the dog dies!" This is NOT true. Life starts NOW. Give the dog a commuted sentence! If you are going to wait for all the stars to align before you do the things you really want to do, you'll NEVER do them.

COMMIT first and then DWIT.

So who is an entrepreneur? He/she is that person you see standing at the back of the line when his/her company is writing checks. My business is a VSB, very small business 100% funded and owned by me. Entrepreneurs certainly do own and operate larger organizations, businesses where they still have personal financial risk but where their business is also funded with additional OPM (other people's money). At minimum their own paychecks are funded (guaranteed) while the company is still in business.

Not so with a VSB. I once chatted with an accountant who advised, "Take a weekly paycheck yourself." So I asked, "What if there's not enough money in the checking account?" to which he responded, "Then don't take a paycheck." I'm glad I wasn't paying for that advice! Today I do manage to write myself a weekly paycheck.

Now this is important, very important. WHO are an entrepreneur's family and friends? Whoever they are, this small group of people can make or break an entrepreneur's business. Our family and friends must be a constant source of support, at least emotionally if not financially too. People in general tend to be negative and while comments from them might come from the right place, concern for you, a well placed negative comment from a naysayer can have you in a tailspin. If you are married and/or have family living with you, they MUST buy in to what you are doing. In terms of success for your business it is better to have no spouse, than a negative spouse. Financially, having a spouse with a job or career means you might have the luxury of running your business at break-even for quite a while. In my case I have health insurance through my Wife's employment, otherwise I'd be one of the millions in the USA today with no health insurance. Can I afford to pay for my own health insurance? Now? Maybe yes. But during the startup of my business? No! If I had to pay $1000 per month for healthcare instead of $1000 per month for Google Adwords, then my business would not have gotten off the ground.

Ya gotta have goals! nah
Ya gotta have a written business plan! nah again

If you are just starting and you feel you have to write a business plan then triple your projected costs and cut in half your projected revenue. If you still have a viable business plan, then proceed. Have you heard stories about businesses started with a business plan written on a napkin? Well, my business got started with the napkin itself!

A business consultant was once close to screaming in my face, "YOU HAVE TO HAVE A WRITTEN PLAN!" I don't get it? My corporate experience was filled with written plans and written budgets, but I just don't see the need for a written plan for a VSB with one owner. My vision for my business is so clear in my mind that I can taste it! I believe this is a shared trait among all successful entrepreneurs. If you ask one to describe their business, where it came from, where it's at, and where it's going, you'll hear them describe their vision as if it were for real, right now today. If you're procrastinating getting started with your business then yeah, writing a business plan will kick-start you into action. Putting things in writing has a way of doing that. If you need to share your business plan with anyone say, for the purposes of raising money, then yeah, you have to put it in writing. But after you're up and running and don't need to share your plan with anyone?

You don't need a written plan.

For ongoing budget planning what works very well for me is, "spend as little as possible". In my conversations with people in the media who seek my advertising dollar, I'm always asked, "What is your budget?" and I always answer, "It depends on how many orders come in tomorrow!"

In an interview of a successful entrepreneur, he said about himself, "I don't know when I became a 'successful entrepreneur' because it seems like just yesterday I was 'that guy who can't hold a day job'." I can relate to that. I've had only one goal since 1994 when I started pursuing the "American Dream", and that is to NEVER work for someone else again. I'm there and have been for a while. I don't need to create business goals to motivate me nor to guide me along the way. I know what I am doing.

Do you hear that flushing noise?

Even Donald Trump says he's been duped. You'll lose money from spending that just didn't work out the way you thought it would. You'll lose money to vendors who over-promise and under-deliver their services and products. You'll lose money to people who outright steal from you, possibly a partner, accountant, or even a family member. Business owners have told me, "Employees will steal from you, whether it is time, merchandise, or cash". One also added, "I'm just happy that something is left for me!"

Your cost per flush is measured in lost time, energy, and money. As you become more successful you'll find what aggravates you the most is the time you waste with bad situations. My time is extremely valuable to me. I only have about 20 years left. You've heard "time is money"? At least with money you know when you have none left!

A Husband telephoned us on a Thursday and asked us a frequent Thursday question, "Can I get them tomorrow?" To which my answer was, "Yes, but it's expensive." Without hesitation he responded, "So are a lot of other things you screw up!" I laughed and wrote down his response. A business life is filled with screw ups. Regardless of whose fault, they flush away your money.

I have a dozen or so examples of advertising attempts that just didn't work out, not through the fault of the vendors.

When I created the RealMoneyTree.com I thought, and still do, that I had created the next "Pet Rock". Everybody has somebody in their life who says "money doesn't grow on trees" and here's a gag gift that says "yes it does!"
I spent $7,000 to work with a commercial videographer, professional voice over guy, and then bought 400 minutes of local cable time for the 30 second commercial. The commercial came out great! We got one order, yes one.

$7,000 to acquire one new customer!

I can still hear the flushing noise!

Then there's the over promising and under delivering.

I'm an "old man" of the internet and I know what I am doing for the most part with, for example, Google Adwords. But I don't have the hours in the day to keep up with what's new or what I can do to "optimize" my results. There are many companies who say they will manage Google Adwords for you and get better results than you. One was a local, rather large company and I visited their facility. My cost per conversion was in the $20 to $25 range which then, as now, has me debating whether it's even worth it to gain a customer at this cost. The salesman explained that the person who would actually be managing my account spends all day every day with Google Adwords, so it made sense to me that he probably could do a better job than me. Then he said the account manager thought he could get my conversion cost down to $5, but of course no promises. I specifically told them NOT to go for the "nosebleed section" search terms such as "flowers" where you can spend $5 per click and get zero conversions. I gave them $2,000 which was my average monthly spend and the freedom to do whatever they thought best with the money. They blew through the $2,000 in two weeks and their average cost per conversion was $130! I don't know what they did, but they didn't know what they were doing.

Yes, I heard that flushing noise again.

Whenever I've been at Chamber of Commerce or other business networking functions my conversations with people in a public relations career always revolved around getting the story of JustPaperRose.com into the media. You've probably read lots of stories about "cute" or different successful small businesses. I believe that our business has several different media worthy stories. We've had a few stories printed in media as a result of my own press releases, but nothing particularly noteworthy, nor enough to create a "buzz". So my question to a PR person is, "So basically you write and send press releases to your personal contacts in the media?" to which the response is, "No, it doesn't work that way." It leaves me thinking, "Well, here is another PR person without media contacts."

I got itchy to try PR with a professional, so I called around to local agencies and found one that had about ten employees. In my chat with the owner he mentioned, "All of us come from the industry…we just call on our old friends…" Finally! Someone who might be "connected"? Three months later and $10,000 spent we had not one story in the media and not one commitment for a story in the works. We didn't even get a story in the Ft. Lauderdale Sun Sentinel or Palm Beach Post which were right in our "backyard". I created JustPaperRoses from their actual newspaper banner-heads (they looked GREAT!) and when I asked who to send them to, the PR agency gave me the street addresses of the two newspapers, no contact name. They had no "old friends". No "new friends" either!

There was that flushing noise again!

One positive thing from the PR experience was being introduced to, and having a one-on-one meeting, with Sy Sperling of Hair Club For Men fame, "I'm not just the president, I'm also a client!" He had sold his company and told me "for enough money to last me several lifetimes!" We had a great meeting and I came away with two lessons.

First, Sy told me that you can't depend on public relations to generate customers for you. PR becomes important AFTER you've gained notoriety to add to your mix of marketing and advertising. I wish he had told me this BEFORE I flushed $10,000!

Second, he told me his own "inch of daylight" story. He said that every business can point to *one* thing that made their business spring-board to success. At the time when Hair Club For Men was already a household name, Sy told me he was deeply in debt and closing in on his limit, after which he'd have to call it quits. I don't remember the exact prices he talked about, but for example a man would spend $150 for their service. After about a year or 18 months the hairpiece would start looking bad – nothing lasts forever and after repeated washings, swimming and sun it looked ragged. A friend of the customer might comment, "Why don't you get rid of that mop on your head" and that was the end of a customer. Sy excitedly told me of his change to a $500 price which entitled the customer to a new hairpiece every year for three years. His revenue soared and customers were happier too! More accurately his revenue soared <u>because</u> his customers were happier.

THERE IS NO FREE LUNCH,
THERE IS NO FREE SHIPPING
THERE IS NO FREE CUSTOMER

I blame Amazon.com for duping people into thinking shipping is FREE. If shipping is free then I'd appreciate if someone would notify UPS and ask them to refund the $50,000 we pay them each year!

A very nice feature of the NetSuite.com is we can measure and identify what is called "shopping cart dropout". These are potential customers who create a customer account while at our website, but then for some reason don't complete a purchase. We can email them and ask them why they didn't order. Once I emailed about 50 and received 10 responses all saying shipping was too expensive. Yes, shipping is expensive when an order is needed quickly. Yes, shipping appears to be relatively expensive when only 1 roll of toilet paper or a single-stem of any of our Anniversary roses is the total order. But one response said the shipping ($20) was just as expensive as the item he wanted to buy ($20). He said he would have no problem spending $40 if the same product was $30 and the shipping was $10. So we raised some of our prices and reduced some of our shipping charges and created "free" standard shipping for orders over $60 to encourage larger orders. This tweaking of prices has worked very well, reducing our shopping cart abandonment by 35%!

There will always be people who believe shipping is free.

Customers do not arrive at your business free of charge.

A myth of internet businesses is that customers are "free". All you have to do is get a high ranking for your site when people search for you on Google and customers come to you free of charge. It's a nice theory. At minimum you have to factor in your time or the cost to hire someone who knows what they are doing to search engine optimize (SEO) your site. Your competitors are looking for YOUR customers too! And your competitors are good with SEO!

On May 8, 2000 I received a phone call from a woman with a company called GoTo.com. She explained that they were a search engine directory for commercial businesses where businesses were displayed ranked on how much they bid for a "click", called pay-per-click or PPC. The higher you bid, the higher your ranking would be. I hung up the phone thinking this was a great deal for them and they probably had a back room filled with employees at computers who did nothing but click all day! No, I was assured there was "click control" on the system so you'd only get charged for 1 click per day even if multiple clicks came from the same computer. I signed up and started bidding on six search terms, 1st Anniversary, First Anniversary, 1st Anniversary Gift, First Anniversary Gift, 1st Wedding Anniversary and First Wedding Anniversary. GoTo.com became Overture.com which was then bought by Yahoo to become Yahoo Search Marketing.

A year later I received an email from GoTo.com pointing out their Keyword Tool and I expanded to about 50 search terms. In June 2001 we had 27 orders, followed by 39, 68, 78, and 99 orders for July, August, September and October! We had "liftoff" and it wouldn't have happened without the PPC on GoTo.com. THANKS GoTo/Overture/Yahoo!

On May 2, 2002 I signed up with Google Adwords, again among the earliest users of their PPC. Google's model was similar to Overture's model. In fact Overture initiated a lawsuit claiming patent infringement which was settled for $300 million by Google shortly before Google did their initial public offering. It's a real kink in the works to try to go public while there's an open lawsuit that threatens the basis upon which a company produces its entire revenue.

Both companies, Overture and Google had placement deals with other search engines. Overture had deals with Yahoo and MSN and Google had a deal with AOL. In the early days the deal was that the top three bidders got visibility on their partner sites. This lead to what I called a horse race. All day long, many times per day, I would check my bids to make sure I was in the top three. For the search terms where few were bidding or three or less were "aggressive" bidders, the bids stayed at a reasonable price. But if four or more bidders wanted to be in the top three, it created a "breakaway" pack of four bidders all leapfrogging each other all day long to be in the top three spots. Not too much later both companies changed their deal to now show all their bidders on their partner sites, but it's still smart to bid enough to get on first page search results.

Since September 2001 we have also listed our products on FindGift.com. They also use a PPC model but they fix the bid price and a vendor's rankings go up and down depending on popularity of an item on their site as determined by number of clicks on that item by visitors to their site. A new listing starts in the middle of the pack.

People ask me, "How do people find you?" and the answer is, "By searching search terms." People don't know they are looking for us until they find us! They search using terms like "1st Anniversary Gift" or "paper roses" or hundreds of other terms that might lead to us. We still spend about $25,000 per year on pay per click. Including all our marketing and advertising costs, each new customer costs us about $10. There is NO free customer!

Well okay, there ARE free customers, those who are repeat customers, and those who are referred by a customer. This is such an important part of success because it is expensive to gain a customer the first time. Over time the average cost to acquire a customer drops as a bigger percentage of total orders are by repeat or referred customers. "Word of mouth" marketing always has been and always will be the most cost effective marketing.

Conversion rate, or how many people buy versus how many people shop, is a very important measure. Whether it is visitors to your website, visitors to your bricks-n-mortar store, or visitors to your booth at an arts & crafts show it is really like "kissing your sister" if the visitor goes away without a purchase.

Conversion rate is a measure of your products' salability as well as your salesmanship. When I go to arts & crafts shows, I'm always amazed at how many vendors just sit in their booth and do not engage conversations with prospective customers. Some even look downright unfriendly sitting in a chair giving out "don't bother me" vibes! And many wonder why they are "starving"?

Online a 2% conversion rate of visitors to your site is considered to be great. During the past 12 months (10/1/08 to 9/30/09) with Google Adwords we've had 8,431,235 "impressions" which is the number of times a page was viewed where our ad was on that page. We had 68,139 clicks so 0.81% click-through-rate. Of those clicking through, we had 688 orders, a 1.01% conversion rate.

So of 100 people clicking through to our site, only 1 in a 100 is buying? Does this make sense to you? We have a highly specialized site and only 1 in 100 people searching for an Anniversary gift buy from us? The answer is that most of these clicks are not "eyeballs" but robotic programs (called bots) that click through for various reasons but mainly to harvest email addresses of websites. That's how and why a web business gets spam emails that are close to target for things that might be of interest (or not) to their business. Some PPC users also believe their competitors click on their ads to run up their costs. Whatever the source these are "spurious clicks" that cost you money and have zero possibility of producing a sale.

An interesting comparison for our Google Adwords results is our results from FindGift.com. This gift listing site works as a pre-filter because people visiting FindGift.com are searching for a gift. During the past 12 months with FindGift we've had 3,702,343 impressions and 48,902 click-throughs so 1.32% compared to Google Adword's 0.81% a 63% better click-through. BUT, we also got 1,521 orders through FindGift, for a 3.11% conversion rate, three times the rate of Google Adwords.

You might be wondering how I know where our customers come from and where do we get such precise numbers? It is one of the great benefits of a website business. Visitors and orders can be electronically tagged. Google has a free (yes, it is FREE) service, Google Analytics. You put a piece of their code in your shopping cart and it tracks where visitors come from and whether or not they buy. In addition the NetSuite.com platform has its own ways of tracking data. This ability to precisely measure advertising performance of online ads is powerful. An old quote in the advertising industry is, "Half of all advertising is not effective. Now if we could only figure out which half!" For example, it's very difficult to measure the effectiveness of any print advertising. This is the primary reason you will see ads designed with special offers or offer codes, which then give the advertiser a way to track effectiveness. When we see an order with the $5 off discount code of BOOK (not valid for book orders!) we will know that this book generated a sale, and that you've read this page!

We KNOW which half of our advertising is effective!

Chapter 14
Sleep with your Customers

*"You can have everything in life you want
if you will just help enough other people
get what they want."*
Zig Ziglar

In the brokerage business I started doing well when I learned to ask potential customers, "What can I do to get your business?" When asked, a potential customer will tell you what they want! If you can provide what they want, you gain a new customer. Listen to your customers. Listen to what they say. Learn to listen to what they don't say!

*"You were given 2 ears and 1 mouth.
Use them in that proportion."*
Anonymous

We have thousands of emailed testimonials. I print them and our testimonial in-box is now a stack two feet high weighing about 40 pounds! We solicit feedback by a simple email follow-up on the night of the occasion asking how the recipient liked the gift. We get back thousands of "she cried", "awesome", "you guys rock", "best gift ever", "I was her hero", "priceless", "magical", etc., testimonials. A lot of our responses start off with "Wow, a company that really cares!" It's an incredible way to start my morning, 6:00 a.m. reading a new batch of testimonials saying great things about us. We also get customer comments and suggestions that are criticisms of one sort or another.

We listen.

In the early days we used a photographic return address label on our shipping box. I figured anyone seeing the box could end up being a customer. One customer commented, "How can I keep this a secret from my Wife when you put a picture of it on the shipping box?" From that moment we've shipped "stealth" in a brown corrugated shipping box with no markings and we even change our return address name to JPR, Inc. Many customers now thank us for shipping "stealth"!

"Most importantly - you kept your word. It arrived fast and was received most appreciatively. Will tell all I have a chance to and look forward to another gift in the future. Ron--------."
^^^ From a customer who ordered by telephone and his top concern was getting his order delivered in two days. I promised him that we, and UPS, would deliver! We did!

We had quite a few customers ask if they could buy a bouquet of 1-stem of each year up to whichever year they are currently celebrating. We've always said "yes" but never had the option available on the website. This year we added this option. For whatever year a customer is celebrating there is a menu choice on our site for 1-stem of each year going backwards to paper. The intent of someone just finding us past their 1st year is that from now on they'll come back each year and add that year's 1-stem to their growing bouquet. As long as their marriage survives, it's almost a guaranteed 1-stem sale each year creating another multiple repeat customer.

Speaking of repeat customers, we even have at least one customer who is now ordering from us for his second Wife! We outlasted his first Wife! We'll be here for his third too!

The #1 question asked by shoppers either by email or telephone is a shipping question. The answers are on the website but it comes down to a customer wanting to know "…how much will it cost me to get it here by (day/date)…" The customer really doesn't want to know when it will be shipped *from* us or what service we use. Most of our customers need day specific delivery within 7 days from ordering. Our website offers the choices, for example if today is Monday: "deliver Tuesday, deliver Wednesday, deliver Thursday, deliver Friday, deliver ON next Monday, deliver AFTER next Monday." The website displays the appropriate delivery date and the shipping charge too.

We've had a lot of testimonials thanking us for the day specific delivery as many customers are sending a gift to their spouse at work on the day of their Anniversary. UPS gets a big THANK YOU for making this happen.

Sleep with your customers. Know them intimately. No, not literally although that could certainly be fun too! I tried this just once and now she's my Wife! I believe the biggest mistake of many marketing professionals is that they confuse their own view of their products or services with the view of customers or potential customers. It's dangerous to think that you personally know what the customer wants. When I'm in the design or redesign mode of a product I lose the ability to judge the outcome. I created it, so I like it. But will the customer like it? One of the best features of an internet business is we can quickly and cheaply find out what sells and what doesn't. Results have surprised me a few times, especially with our toilet paper! LISTEN to your customers and to your business and you will always learn something new. We are always students of Entrepreneurship. We never graduate!

You most likely are a customer of your business and certainly its biggest fan! Our biggest group of customers is Husbands buying our products for an Anniversary gift for their Wives. We help him with romance on the eve of his Anniversary and hopefully he gets what he wants that night! So how isn't this me? I'm a romantic gift giver type of guy and always have been. Why am I not the profile of our typical customer? Because, I've never had to *buy* our products. I've never been through the buying decision.

Ya can't please all of the people all of the time.

This is a Universal Principle and every business has returns and disappointed customers. Ours is no exception, BUT our return rate is about 1/3 of 1% or 1 in 300 orders. The typical retail store has about 7% returns and has a "returns department" or even a warehouse devoted to "returns". Handling returns is very expensive, more money flushed. Our returns are primarily because the Husband didn't get the anticipated reaction, which is usually because: 1) the couple just had a fight about money and agreed not to spend money on each other for their Anniversary, and/or 2) the Wife is pragmatic about gifts and doesn't click with the romanticism or the thoughtfulness of her Husband.

A few of our returns were very disappointed with the product and stated in one way or another that what they received looks NOTHING like what is on our website. They feel ripped off, bait and switched. One even emailed a photo of his order of JustWoodRoses and wrote, "see?" But no, I didn't see because his photo looked just like our photo online. Why would we sell something different than what is pictured online? I don't get it.

We even had one woman email us, "I would like to return this item, it is not what I thought it would look like. How do I go about returning it?" Her purchase? Our toilet paper printed with "Happy 1st 'paper' Anniversary". She added, "I didn't like the product at all." I didn't have the courage to ask her, "What did you think a printed roll of toilet paper would look like, other than what is photographed online?"

With the exception of glitches or damage by UPS, or glitches by us, unfavorable product reception almost always is going to come down to customers' expectation. Usually that word is right in their complaint, "…not what I expected." Somehow their expectations are beyond what they are seeing and reading at the website. When a customer is NOT pleased, at minimum you can and should do everything possible to erase any negative feelings they might have about you and your business. At maximum you can turn the unhappy customer into a happy customer.

The key to responding to an unhappy customer is:

> **First, respond quickly.**
> **Second, take ownership of the problem.**
> **Third provide a remedy.**

I sit in front of my computer screen all day and it's not unusual for me to respond to any email as soon as it's received. We get back a lot of "Wow, thanks for the quick response." If it is our or UPS's glitch my response starts with, "Our apology for our (or for UPS's) glitch" and if appropriate, "We'll ship you a replacement of your order today, at no charge of course." If a customer wants a refund, we refund the full purchase price and sometimes, depending on circumstances, shipping costs too.

Glitches will happen. Nobody has a 0% glitch rate. We have a very small number of UPS delivery glitches and a very small number of our own glitches. We're lightening quick at an attempt to recover from a glitch.

If the customer says a package is not there when it is supposed to be, we first do the UPS tracking. Many times UPS tracking shows UPS did deliver and package left at side door or garage. Or, tracking shows the package is sitting in the company mailroom. We tell this to the customer and 5 minutes later they usually thank us and tell us they have the package. Sometimes a package is not found even though UPS says it delivered. About half of these are quickly found because it was delivered to a neighbor who was kind enough to redeliver. The other half are usually never found. But remember, this is a very small number. We tell our customers that UPS glitch rate is very small and we also know that knowing this doesn't help much when it's YOUR package that was delayed or lost. If it's a question of having a product in hand tomorrow, we ship a replacement overnight at no charge. Our response to glitches have even brought testimonials and resulted in a happy customer likely to buy again from us in the future. Respond quickly, take ownership, and provide a remedy.

Your customers do not want to spend a lot of time nor get lost in the shopping process. A very helpful book for website design is "Don't Make Me Think!" by Steve Krug. We're on our 5th website but from the very beginning I've tried to "dummy down" the website. We still get the question once every month or two about a shipping choice that would for example say "Deliver on Wednesday 9/30". The question asked is "Does that mean it's the day the order is delivered or is that the day you ship the order?

How we could make it any clearer? Suggestions?

We've tried to keep the option choices for products to a minimum. More options and variations require more thinking by a shopper. That doesn't necessarily mean there should be no choices but when there are, such as selecting color, number of stems or adding a vase, the process of making these choices should be quite simple. We have menu choices in dropdown menus and our site is visual. See a product? Click to buy! We keep wording to a minimum and use simple descriptive words.

"It's the little things that count." Well, ALL things count and in many cases the little things really don't make much of a difference, but we do them anyway. We gift wrap all our TP orders with green tissue, ribbons and a gift card and we don't even mention on our website that we do this gift wrapping. Many of our customers ship to themselves and then switch the TP in their bathroom for a surprise gag, but even then, the gift wrapped presentation when they open the box creates a great first impression of our company.

Many of our repeat customers order forgetting to use their discount code for being a repeat customer. When we check in orders and see it's a repeat customer we apply the code, charging them $5 less than they thought they spent.

Occasionally we have a customer ask, "Can I place an order today but not have it charged until my Anniversary date so my Wife doesn't see the charge on our account?" We say "yes." The same for the occasional customer who wants to send a check because they have no credit card.

All of our packaging and products are designed to survive UPS shipping, more a necessity than a little thing. Twice per month a prospective customer will ask, "Are you sure these will get here in one piece?" After 30,000 shipments worldwide, yes we are sure. And for that rare time when UPS puts a 50 pound package on top of ours? We replace damaged orders quickly and at no charge.

A few customers even forget which year Anniversary they are celebrating! Now why do I know that this doesn't surprise you? With repeat customers we take a quick look at their order history and more than a few times we have prevented a customer from making a BIG mistake:

"thanks it was great. and thanks again for correcting my mistake on the years that I have been married. my wife said i would have been in trouble if i would have gotten it wrong. thanks again ya'll really saved me !!!!!!!!!!!!!!!!!!! until next time."

The saying "the devil is in the details" means the small details of something makes it difficult or challenging. Master the details of your business and you will have a masterful business! Our biggest compliment is when a customer tells us we are "dialed in" to our business!

Our day specific delivery creates a good impression even for those not needing day specific delivery. Let's say today is Monday. A customer who is shipping to themselves (so they can give the gift personally) and needs their order beyond 7 days from now sees the non-expedited shipping choices of "Deliver ON (next) Monday (month/date)" and "Deliver AFTER (next) Monday (month/date)", and they are the same price. Most choose the ON option and *ON* next Monday their first impression of our service is, "well, they said it would be delivered on Monday, and here it is, ON Monday!" We deliver to whatever shipping address is provided, hotels, restaurants, or even Mom's house to hide the gift. While this is standard practice for us and most gift companies, it's another "little thing" customers appreciate.

We offer FREE shipping to APO/FPO military addresses which means the gift is being shipped to a soldier on active duty. We do this simply because it's the right "little thing" to do to help out our military families. It's even a nice "little thing" for all of our customers to see, as it reflects well on our business. We have LOTS of bouquets in Iraq and testimonials too that say our soldiers really appreciate our 2-ply toilet paper, no matter what is printed on it!

Selling ON purpose follows sleeping with your customer. Selling ON purpose can be translated two ways. First it means selling that is laser focused on the purpose of your business and the reason a customer buys from you. For us it is "to help create a great Anniversary celebration". This is what we do, our mission statement. Second it means to sell not by accident, but on purpose. Do not just put your stuff "out there" and see what sells (throw it against the wall and see what sticks?). We've had over 30,000 customers and it didn't just happen by accident. We take many purposeful steps to guide the potential customer first to us, and then through their purchasing decision.

People LOVE to buy, but they HATE to be sold. You help your customers buy when you sell ON purpose!

Do YOU have a unique selling proposition? Ours spins off of the traditions of "themes" for Wedding Anniversaries. Our customers want to buy something made from this year's material. We further define our uniqueness by creating flowers with those materials. If these material themes did not exist, our business would not exist.

How much candy would be sold if it were not for Halloween, Valentine's Day and Easter? How many fruitcakes would be sold if it were not for Christmas? How many religious items would be sold if it were not for religious traditions? The list is long. Take an "out of the box" look at your own interests and see if there are ways your product or service can be marketed ON a tradition.

What makes your product and/or service unique? Do you know WHY people buy your product or service? Our customers buy from us because they are seeking a romantic or humorous reaction from their spouse or other recipient. Do you know WHY people buy from you and not your competitors? In our case we have no direct competitor, but if we did it would be our presentation, delivery, follow-up and customer service that makes us #1.

Sleep with your customers, zzzzzzzzzzzzzzzzzzzz

Chapter 15
Where do I go from Here?

"Don't confuse a clear view with a short distance."
Paul Saffo

I am so very guilty of confusing them. My view for the future of my business and my life is so crystal clear that I can smell and taste it. It should be here…RIGHT NOW!

"You can't push a river."
Buddhist proverb
(thank you Victoria)

I used to have conversations where I would say, "I want to build the business to $1 million in annual sales and then sell out to a larger floral company, like 800-Flowers or FTD, or to a short list of large gift companies." One wise businessman replied, "When your business does $1 million in annual sales, you **won't** want to sell out." His point was that at the $1 million level I'll be making all the money I need or want. Like my Dad in the 1950's, I'd be making more money than I can spend. We're not there yet. My byline is,

> We've had 30,000 customers but
> NOBODY knows about us!

Ten years from now I'd like to say,

> We've had 3,000,000 customers and
> EVERYBODY knows about us!

I have stopped soliciting bigger companies for a buyout or partnership. If it happens it will be by them finding me.

In 2001 I got to the right department at Coca-Cola, the department that sends out their corporate gifts. We created a few bouquets of white JustPaperRoses printed with the red Coca-Cola logo. We package all our products in clear long-stem rose boxes with tissue, ribbons and glitter, so our standard presentation to Coke looked great. We raised the bar by using an empty Coke can and a plastic Coke bottle instead of vases. They looked GREAT! We received a note, handwritten, expressing how wonderful they looked and, "…rest assured you will get lots of orders from us". Eight years later, I'm still resting. Not one order.

I've lost track of how many companies I cold solicited, sending JustPaperRoses printed with their company logo. Without exception the presentation looks great. Without exception we've received no response. Granted I don't do a follow up call, but I finally learned to not cold solicit.

We have had a few very nice corporate orders, but they were all from people who found us.

Two weeks before Valentine's Day 2007 we received a phone call from an advertising company asking if we could make JustPaperRoses from Budweiser beer labels. They sent a few labels in overnight mail and I quickly figured out how to tape together two labels and some white paper to give us the size we needed to make a JustPaperRose. We overnighted the samples back and quickly got the "go" for 500 Budweiser JustPaperRoses and we received over 1000 labels a few days later. Budweiser was the sponsor for the Sports Illustrated Swimsuit Edition Valentine's Day party at a nightclub in New York City. 500 women were given a Budweiser JustPaperRose! I was invited to attend the party too! When I told my Wife about the invite she informed me that attending a party with all those swimsuit models might be fatal for a man with my "condition".

"Funny" because I had no idea I even had a "condition"!

A photo of the Budweiser JustPaperRoses is on our home page of the website. We have had customers ask if we can make those for them, but the answer is "no" because we only create logo JustPaperRoses for the owner of the logo.

Domtar is a huge Canadian paper company. They contacted us to see if we could make our small Origami Orchids as centerpieces, using their own Domtar paper, for their Las Vegas company meeting. They overnighted us the paper and they came out GREAT!

We've also created centerpieces for Kodak, made with a new photo paper they printed with bright red roses. Their event was the introduction of this new photo paper.

We've had 20 or so corporate orders and each was unique and creative using their logos and/or colors. We've had some very small orders from some very large companies! And again, they were ALL orders by people who found us and none from companies I had cold solicited.

I'm always asked about 800-Flowers and FTD. Usually the conversation starts with, "Don't you worry about a big company copying you?" To which I respond, "Big companies really aren't looking to steal ideas and besides, they can buy me out cheap! Also, I've already offered myself to them and they just don't 'get it'."

I've had three approaches with 800-Flowers. The first time my products were introduced by another of their vendors. After a few weeks of phone calls trying to connect to the right person, I got through. The woman was slurring her words and since this was just after lunch I assumed she drank her lunch. She said with a condescending tone, "We have no interest AT ALL in your products."

A few years later I called on them again and followed their instructions to send a sample and information. If you call on a big business every two or three years, the chances are good you'll be dealing with someone new, not the person who turned you down previously. This time an assistant to the right person returned my follow-up call and she said she had the sample bouquet in her hands. She asked, "Do you have a website?" which obviously meant my cover letter and business card was not with the sample in her hands. Also it meant she had no idea of what we do. She asked, "How much do you get for these?" and I replied, "$55". Her response? "OH NO, we get $29.95 for a dozen fresh roses." HUH ??? I felt like replying, "Honey, $29.95 is our GROSS MARGIN!"

My third encounter with 800-FLOWERS was in the spring of 2007 when a VP called me. We had a few discussions but it never went anywhere. He said he couldn't stir up interest in the Anniversary niche in his office.

Granted (and thankfully) it is a very small niche.

Similarly I've had two approaches to FTD. The first time I was turned down with a snooty, "OUR customers won't buy these!" I didn't know what to say. FTD's customers ARE our customers, aren't they? Our customers buy fresh flowers too! When they want fresh flowers they use a traditional florist. The second time I got a response of, "We tried something like that before and it didn't work." HUH??? At that point we had 20,000 customers and I included that info in my cover letter. It works…for us!

I've also contacted 40 or 50 other mid-size floral and/or gift companies even to just suggest partnering, with our products selling through their businesses, and have had zero interest.

I think what happens is the person on the receiving end feels it is his or her job description to figure out whether or not our products will sell. They seem to look at our products as a sample prototype and also as a replacement for fresh roses. It made no difference that my cover letters stated we had cumulative sales of 10,000 or 20,000 customers. It made no difference that our testimonials are all over the top with many "...she cried...". It made no difference that we were discussing a unique product that their competitor(s) don't have. It made no difference that many of our customers tell us they first asked their local florist if they had paper roses for a 1st Anniversary and found us after the local florist lost a sale.

At this writing we've had over 30,000 customers and have passed the $2 million mark in cumulative (10 years) sales. It is well beyond a "given" that our products sell. Plus it is relatively easy to date before marriage. A partner approach puts our products on their site(s) for a short test run so they can see for themselves whether or not their customers will buy our products and at what volume.

So, I've stopped thinking about doing anything with a bigger company. In their defense, a big company really doesn't want to look at a company like ours until it passes the $1 million mark in annual sales, preferably $10 million.

There is no such thing as a *silent* partner!

Several times I've had conversations with Jay "contemplating" an investment in my business by him and/or his partners. Like my comments on suicide, contemplating is a step below planning which is a step below doing. So many of us with start-up businesses, or with business ideas still on the drawing board, think other people's money (OPM) is the solution, the only solution, and the "missing link" for success. How many times do you hear someone who is broke say something like, "If I only had $5 million, this business (or business idea) would make a billion!" My own interest in OPM has always been for money to be spent on advertising. For example, I'd like to advertise on AskMen.com. Their minimum spend is $10K per month, preferably $15K, and a proper campaign should go for a minimum of six months, preferably a year. So I'd spend at minimum $60K, at maximum $180K. Myself? I can afford it *if* I'm right, and *if* the results are immediate.

But I can't afford it if I'm wrong.
I don't want to hear that flushing noise again!

NOW it would be somebody else's money. If I lost Jay's money I wouldn't be able to sleep at night. And there's no such thing as a silent partner. People who put THEIR money into your business are smarter than you! How do I know this? Because *they* have the money you seek! At minimum they've been doing what they've been doing longer than you have. Jay has a 25 year head-start on me.

Plus, for me, my only objective is to NEVER work for someone else again. Jay saying "no" to his possible involvement with my business means today I still own 100% of my company.

THANKS Jay, for just saying "no"!

So where do I go from here? I want to help 3,000,000 Husbands and Wives celebrate their Anniversaries with romance, joy and laughter. We've received thousands of testimonials. This is our favorite, from a repeat customer:

"I had to change thing up a bit this year. She is now 'expecting' the roses. She tells everyone about them. As you know it was our "Fruit" anniversary this year. I knew she was taking the day off, so I had her other fruity gift delivered to her at work the day before our anniversary. That gift was a big hit, all her friends were jealous. She came home a bit on the depressed side. She thought I wasn't getting her the roses this year. Money has been tight so she thought I sent everything early and that was it. WRONG. I had to work on our anniversary, so when I came home, I went upstairs and brought her down her Fruit Roses. Can you say waterworks? She loved them. The look on her face was priceless. What struck me the most was how much she missed them the day before. I was already thinking that maybe after the three years of getting them that they were getting old, and expected. Well, I was half right, she was expecting them, but they are definitely not getting old. Thank you very much for another great gift. I'm sure you get these comments all the time, but I just had to let you know. Keep up the great work. Ed N." 10/18/09

Wow! Waterworks!!!

Do YOU know ANY Husband who would like to get this type of reaction from his Wife on their Anniversary?

Do you know any Husband who would **NOT** like this type of reaction??? If so, take his pulse and call 911.

PLEASE tell, call, or email ALL your married friends and family to tell them about us. Especially, think of any Wedding you've attended or been invited to in the past year. Think of that Groom now Husband as he approaches his 1st "paper" Anniversary with the fear of having to find his first ever Anniversary gift for his Wife. YOU can "save the day" for him! If the Bride now Wife is your best contact then tell her about our 1st Anniversary TP!

We have the first 19 years of Anniversaries covered so please refer us to ANY married couple, either a Husband or a Wife, but not both – it would ruin the surprise!

So where do I go from here? I want to grow our business to the $1 million+ in annual sales.

I also want to help people who don't know what they want to be when they grow up. If you believe that this book can inspire someone in your life, then please buy them a book as a gift from you to him or her.

Do you know 12 people who need inspiration?

We discount by the dozen!

Chapter 16
Make your Bed

"Make your bed."
Anonymous

At the very worst time of my life a man asked me, "Do you make your bed every morning?" I replied, "No." He added, "How do you think you're going to turn your life around if you can't even manage to make your bed?"

"Early to bed, early to rise,
makes a man healthy, wealthy, and wise."
Ben Franklin

Now, I make my bed every morning!

Is this a literal or metaphorical instruction? Well, both.
One's bedroom should be a sanctuary, a place in your
house where you can relax and get away from everything
outside your sanctuary. Walking into your bedroom at
night and seeing a made bed is a very nice thing.

Make your bed. But also, it is metaphorical.

"You've made your bed and now you have to sleep in it"

usually is a comment about a negative situation. But what
if I've made a very nice bed? Do I still get to sleep in it?

If you're not happy with a part or all of your life, then you
have to start, right NOW, doing things to start moving in
your desired direction. To start, do small things differently,
like making your bed, reading a good book instead of
watching TV, or finally cleaning out the garage.

The start of turning a hobby into a business is simply to do
more and more of your hobby, spending more hours doing
what you enjoy doing anyway. What do you enjoy doing?
What would you do with your time if you didn't have to
make money doing it? Several times when I've had a
"do what you love" conversation with a group of people
there's always one guy who says, "I love to go to the beach
and drink beer!" and everybody chuckles. I respond, "No,
nobody is going to pay you to go to the beach and get
drunk, but have you ever heard of a guy named Ron Rice?"

I continue, "He was a lifeguard, going to the beach every day. He mixed 50 gallon drums of his own recipe for suntan lotion, bottled it himself, and sold it from the trunk of his car. When he opened his Hawaiian Tropic factory it was a block away from the ocean so he and his employees could go to the beach on Friday afternoons!"

And I add, "How about those Sam Adams commercials? WOW, now these guys are dedicated to beer. The beer industry is ALWAYS looking for people who are dedicated to brewing and marketing beer. Or better yet, open your own microbrewery right across the street from a beach!"

Whether you don't know what you want to be when you grow up, or just want to turn your hobby into a nice side business, the answer is to do your hobby more and more.

In his book "Outliers" Malcolm Gladwell writes that the commonality among all people who are at the top of what they do is that they had 10,000 hours of practice before they even got to the starting line. 10,000 hours seems to be a consistent observation. Before Bill Gates started MicroSoft he had 10,000 hours of time on computers. Before Tiger Woods became a pro he had played 10,000 hours of golf. 10,000 hours is 20 hours per week for 10 years and not easy to achieve in less than 10 years.
I figure I've just passed the 10,000 hour mark of actively making our products, 10,000 hours of finger time!

YOUR 10,000 hours starts…RIGHT NOW!
See you in 10 years?

If you don't currently have a hobby or interest that inspires you but "have always wanted to try…" then start NOW! If you rarely do your hobby then step on the accelerator and do it more. If you're actively doing your hobby then tweak up the volume and **put your hobby on steroids!**

I DON'T HAVE TIME,
IT'S HARD WORK
I'M NOT CREATIVE

These are your three biggest enemies and if you are like me, they've taken up residence between your ears. You DO have time, 24 hours each and every day. But if you don't think you have time, then what you are saying is that having your dream job or business, your dream life, is just a dream for you because it's not a priority for your time.

Hard work? Unless your dream includes heavy manual labor there is NOTHING hard about any work. Whenever I hear someone compliment someone as a "hard worker", or "she worked hard to get to where she is", I reply with, "it is NOT 'hard' work, it is *diligent* work." Would you hesitate doing more and more of what you like to do only because it would require diligent work?

You ARE creative and I know that for a fact! Don't tell me I'm wrong. EVERYONE is creative but most of us have not exercised our creativity since we left the playground. PLAY with whatever you enjoy doing. What do you do that brings a great reaction from people around you? Do more of it. YOU are creative!

We sell retail directly to our customers, but this is certainly not the only way to go. For example, we have six vendors of products who are in the category of crafters: wood vases, leather roses, bloodwood roses, pottery roses, steel roses, and tagua nut roses. These vendors all sell through traditional arts & craft shows. We are the "bread & butter" type of wholesale customer for them, with a steady volume of sales. Last year we sold 714 wood vases! Our vase crafter has three other wholesale relationships. He said his volume is now "more than this one man army can handle!" He's another home hobbyist with a "hobby on steroids"! Our biggest years are 1, 2, 3, 5, 10 and 15, or paper, cotton, leather, wood, aluminum, and crystal. I'm always looking for great ideas or products in these materials. I'd "kill" to find an artist who can make a "killer" crystal rose.

A hurdle with most arts & crafters is getting a high enough price just to compensate for their time spent making their product. When wholesaling your art or craft, you need to be able to make a profit at half of the retail price. It becomes crucial for you to figure out efficient ways to create your product without compromising quality.

"Do what you love" does NOT have to be arts and crafts, or a hobby. It can be anything you enjoy doing. The good news is that to be successful with your own small business you do not have to invent something new. If you are in or want to be in a type of business that already exists there is more good news – all you have to do is be better than your competition. And ready for the best news?

Your competition does not set the bar very high!

In Florida, more than one service company advertises "WE SHOW UP", also lettered on their trucks. Amazing. Simply showing up puts them ahead of their competitors! Very sad. Very true. Can YOU show up?

The products that sell best are the ones that have a function or fill a need in a unique way. Look for the busiest booths at an arts & crafts show. They're ALWAYS the artists or crafters who make women's jewelry, handbags, and clothes. Fashionable and artsy, but with a function too! Women ALWAYS buy jewelry, handbags, and clothes!

Immerse yourself in what you want to do, and then figure out why ONE customer buys from you. Then go find thousands more customers, just like that one customer.

Marketing is all about perceived value. What is your perceived value of yourself? How much are YOU worth?

We all manifest our own future and it's based on what is going on between our ears at this very moment. Today's thinking becomes tomorrow's reality. We become what we think. I live with what I call "fuzzy manifestation". I do not meditate nor write down any specific goals. Okay, the black Corvette photo on my desk was *very* specific! But, my "fuzzy manifestation" started many years ago with two very unspecific, very fuzzy visions:

1) I want my own business.
2) I want a GREAT primary relationship (marriage).

I now have JustPaperRoses, Inc., and my Wife Deb.

There IS a place in this world for someone like me,
a man who can make beautiful flowers with his fingers!

"It" happened to me.
"It" can happen to you.

*"Life is like a roll of toilet paper.
The closer you get to the end,
the faster it goes."*

Suggested Reading

I subscribe to the "one thing" philosophy for reading, listening to a speaker, or having a conversation or lunch with a person of interest. If I come away with one thing learned, then it was well worth my time, energy, and money. Many of my stories are "one thing" stories put together here to create a "lots of things" book.

I hope you've gained "one thing" from reading my book.

My suggested reading list is ridiculously short and not meant to be complete. For my selected authors who are prolific, several of their books in addition to the one I mention can be helpful. These twelve books represent a focus of improving one's own life, all from slightly or not so slightly different perspectives.

194

In order of date written or published:

1) Tao Te Ching by Lao Tsu about 2500 years ago.
I like the version by Gia-Fu Feng and Jane English ©1989.
Loosely translated as "the way" or "the path", Tao Te Ching
is an easy to read 81 pages of "poems" that will have you
learning something new with each reading. My biggest
"one thing" from my reading and rereading of this book, is
that people are the same today as we were 2500 years ago.
The wisdom and guidance for achieving a happy and
successful life has not changed throughout the ages.

2) Think & Grow Rich by Napolean Hill ©1960.
Considered to be the cornerstone of the self-help movement,
this book was among the first to chronicle the philosophy of
 "you are what you think".

3) The Tao Jones Averages by Bennett Goodspeed ©1983.
The byline is "a guide to whole-brained investing" His book is
"dedicated to everyone who has the guts to follow his gut."

4) Way of the Peaceful Warrior by Dan Millman ©1980.
While the story is a fictionalized account of the author's
experiences, his story mirrors many "I can't explain this"
things that have happened in my life.

5) A Whack on the Side of the Head by Roger von Oech ©1983.
A Kick in the Seat of the Pants (of course) ©1986.
Whether you are at the beginning, middle, or end of your
creative career, these books will fire up your creative juices!

6) Fighting to Win by David Rogers ©1984.
"Samurai techniques for your work and life."
This book is a wonderful adaptation of ancient Samurai
techniques and wisdom applied to the western world of today.

7) The E-Myth Revisited by Michael Gerber ©1995.
A **must** read for anyone who is "good at something" and wants to turn it into a business. "E" stands for Entrepreneur and the author chronicles the three phases of a business – technician, where you do what you are good at, for 16 hours per day; then manager, where you hire people to do what you are good at and you manage them; and finally business owner, where you manage your managers.

8) Manifest Your Destiny by Wayne Dyer ©1997.
Do YOU want a Corvette in your garage? Wayne will guide you through the process of choreographing your own life.

9) KISS and Make-Up by Gene Simmons ©2001.
Okay, you're probably laughing. I had NO idea of whom KISS or Gene Simmons were when they were onstage, other than a band of crazy guys dressed up in outrageous costumes and painted faces. This book is about MARKETING, about selling ON purpose! Nothing about Gene's Simmons' KISS happened by accident. He's a "crab with good marketing"!

10) Shut Up, Stop Whining, & Get A Life by Larry Winget ©2004.
Wow! His byline is "A Kick-Butt Approach to a Better Life." If Larry can't wake you up and get you moving, then you are dead! BUY (and read) THIS BOOK!

11) Lucky or Smart? By Bo Peabody ©2005.
Too often I hear comments about successful entrepreneurs that include "he just got lucky." Do YOU feel lucky today?

12) Outliers by Malcolm Gladwell ©2008.
A fascinating book revealing that the true story of success is NOT about intelligence and ambition. It's about practice!